THE Naughty COOK BOOK

DECADENT
RECIPES TO
SEDUCE
YOUR
TASTE BUDS

THE Naughty COOK BOOK

SAMANTHA SCHNUR

Creator of @thenaughtyfork

PHOTOGRAPHS BY LAUREN VOLO

CLARKSON POTTER/PUBLISHERS
NEW YORK

CLARKSON POTTER/PUBLISHERS
An imprint of the Crown Publishing Group
A division of Penguin Random House LLC
1745 Broadway
New York, NY 10019
clarksonpotter.com
penguinrandomhouse.com

CLARKSON POTTER is a trademark and POTTER with colophon is
a registered trademark of Penguin Random House LLC.

Library of Congress Cataloging-in-Publication Data
Names: Schnur, Samantha [author]
Title: The naughty cookbook: decadent recipes to seduce
    your taste buds / Samantha Schnur.
Description: First edition. | New York: Clarkson Potter/
    Publishers, [2026] | Includes index.
Identifiers: LCCN 2025011694 | ISBN
    9780593799697 hardback | ISBN 9780593799703 ebook
Subjects: LCSH: Cooking | LCGFT: Cookbooks
Classification: LCC TX714 .S373 2026 | DDC 641.5—dc23/
    eng/20250416
LC record available at https://lccn.loc.gov/2025011694

ISBN 978-0-593-79969-7
Ebook ISBN 978-0-593-79970-3

Editor: Layla Schlack | Assistant editor: Bri James
Production designer: Christina Self
Production editors: Liana Faughnan and Patricia Shaw
Production: Kim Tyner | Art director: Stephanie Huntwork
Compositors: Merri Ann Morrell and Hannah Hunt
Food stylist: Mira Evnine
Prop stylist: Maeve Sheridan
Co-writer: Laura Arnold
Copy editor: Kate Slate | Proofreaders: Eldes Tran,
Hope Clarke, Sigi Nacson, Nancy Inglis, and Miriam Taveras
Indexer: Elizabeth Parson
Publicist: Jana Branson | Marketer: Stephanie Davis

Manufactured in China

10 9 8 7 6 5 4 3 2 1

First Edition

The authorized representative in the EU for product safety
and compliance is Penguin Random House Ireland, Morrison
Chambers, 32 Nassau Street, Dublin D02 YH68, Ireland,
https://eu-contact.penguin.ie.

FOR MY DAD AND BEST FRIEND:

There has been no greater joy in my life than the privilege of calling you my father. Because of the man you are, I've spent every day striving to live up to your example and make you proud.

From the very start, you've been my rock—cheering me on when I chose a path less certain (like leaving premed to pursue food photography) and trusting me when I barely trusted myself. You believed in me before there was anything to believe in. Your strength, love, and constant encouragement have carried me through every doubt, every challenge, every step of this journey.

You are more than my biggest supporter—you're the person I look up to, the one whose pride means the world to me. This cookbook is a tribute to all the little moments we've shared—the four-times-a-day phone calls, the pickleball matches, the endless dinners and lunches, and the belly laughs—that showed me how love can build something beautiful.

This book wouldn't exist without you. Thank you for giving me the courage to chase my dreams and for being the best dad (and taste-tester) I could ever ask for. Can you believe it, Pops? I made it!!!

This one's for you.

Contents

INTRODUCTION

Let's cook NAUGHTY.

The kitchen is my playland, an oasis to let my inhibitions go, get creative, and try new things. I'm always looking for the next way to level up a sandwich, transform a complex restaurant dish into an approachable meal at home, or mash up the latest flavor craze into a thoughtful yet decadent recipe. A great meal arouses all sorts of pleasurable feelings, and my philosophy is to chase those. And these qualities, my friends, are what define a dish as *naughty*.

YOU MAY RECOGNIZE ME from my social media channel @thenaughtyfork. I've built my whole brand and professional identity on the desire to expose food at its most sumptuous. Whether it be a cheese pull, drip of sauce or egg yolk, or placing the cherry on top, there's a true moment of extravagance in every recipe, and it's my goal to highlight it. My channel started out over ten years ago as a place to showcase insane restaurant dishes from all over the world. Flash forward to 2020, the pandemic hit, and my content shifted. This was the pivotal moment for me and the Naughty brand. It's when I began getting down and dirty in the kitchen, teaching myself how to make decadent creations to share with all of you. It started with re-creating restaurant meals for my home kitchen that we were all longing for during quarantine. And at first, I struggled. I can't tell you the number of times I've smoked up my kitchen, left something to toast under the broiler for too long, or burned the tips of my fingers from pulling apart piping hot sandwiches. But it was all so worth it, since today my platform is primarily a place where I share my own personally developed recipe creations and viral trends that have come to life, like the smashed croissant sandwich and smash burger tacos.

When it comes to my audience, I love you all. You inspire me daily to live my dream job and to always think naughty. It's my community that gives me ideas of what recipe I should develop next, viral concepts everyone loves, and the excitement to elevate sinful dishes for your viewing pleasure. Ever since I began honing my cooking skills as a self-taught chef a few years ago, the support and motivation from the Naughty community has been incredible. Everything from my love of sandwiches, to your love of all things carbs, the creation of the smash burger taco, and so many more, my culinary think tank is endless.

After three years of developing recipes for my platform, I felt like it was time to share a collection of my classic and new recipes in writing with all of you, and so *The Naughty Cookbook* was born. The answer to why I wrote this cookbook hit me: I can't wait for you to be able to cook and share these recipes with me from your own home kitchens and not just through the lens of social media. It's a form of connection that as an influencer is sometimes hard to find.

Some of you have known me, for many years, as an over-the-top food creator who likes to make a dish shine on camera. But with this cookbook, I'm so excited to establish a deeper connection with you and my community to further share my obsession of all things indulgent and delicious; I want you to be able to join the Naughty Fork dinner party, too! Entertaining and feeding my friends and family (and really anyone I run into) is my number one hobby. It brings me the most joy to see everyone around a table enjoying my recipes and creations. This act of cooking and dining, whether it be at home or in a restaurant, is a show that I know all of you also love to experience. From picking a menu theme, to setting the table, getting dressed up (or not!), and cooking for hours from start to finish, the performance of hosting a meal is my ultimate pleasure. And let me be straight, it doesn't have to be fancy or complicated. These recipes are eaten by everyone, everywhere. Whether I'm filming in my kitchen or developing new content for a brand, my first call is my friends, neighbors, the person I just met in the lobby of my building. If you're hungry, I can't wait to feed you. (It's even gotten to the point of the parking attendants in my building calling me "Miss Cookie" after I've given them so many leftovers.) For these exact reasons, I wanted to take my ideas and recipes from my channel and gather them into one glamorous book so mealtime can feel like a luxury.

I'm part of the club that lives to eat rather than eats to live, and I eat through more ways than just taste. Rather, I use all my senses. I want you to feel the heat of the spicy vodka rigatoni in the back of your throat, and the ultrasmooth texture of the caramelized French onion dip on the tip of your tongue, and make your whole mouth water from the juiciest filet mignon sandwich. Every recipe is built on the idea of layers of flavors and textures. It's how I create my recipes. The idea of heat, crunch, freshness, creaminess, a hint of sweetness, and tart acid are my favorite senses coming out through every bite in my dishes. My mission with *The Naughty Cookbook* is for you to create the greatest mouthful of pleasurable flavors.

The videos on my channel may seem daunting or difficult to even try to re-create at home, but I'll be the first to tell you, if I can do it, so can you. It'll be a messy, delicious experience, and honestly not as difficult to master as you'd think. Just roll up your sleeves and get ready to have fun and make mistakes (like setting off the smoke detector from searing a steak), like I did and still even do. I want *The Naughty Cookbook* to function for you both as a glamorous coffee table book and have several smudge marks and dog-eared pages from playing in the kitchen. My whole goal when it comes to being in the kitchen is flirtatious fun. Whether you're cooking for yourself, a hot new date, or a group of friends and family, it's the ultimate sign of compassion and love anyone will appreciate. So go pick a recipe, grab those ingredients, and let's cook *naughty*.

MY STORY

Let's rewind to how my unique relationship with cooking and restaurants all began at an early age. Being born and raised in Miami, I was lucky to have an eclectic cultural dining scene with all different types of cuisines at my fingertips. Some kids were theater nerds; I geeked out on food—dining out and enjoying the "performance" that a restaurant put on was one of my favorite activities growing up. I came to view a good meal as the ultimate act of self-care, an indulgence no one should deny themselves.

My love of dining out with family and friends in high school led me to experience incredible restaurants, try unique dishes, and meet industry leaders, which only reinforced my interest in the food and beverage industry. When I left Miami to go to college at Florida State University, I quickly reverted to this familiar comfort and hobby of dining out to find good cheap eats and comfort food that would be accessible to other college students like me. I was always at the local pizza spot called Gumby's, trying every new item at Taco Bell, eating chicken fingers at Guthrie's, and frequently caught lunching at Olive Garden. Any new fast casual place was immediately added on my to-do list; you name it, I wanted to try it. I was on a mission of not wanting to be confined to the college cafeteria or a frozen pizza on a Friday night. I began documenting these food adventures in the early days of Instagram with my account @thenaughtyfork, and it was taking off—quickly.

I kept up with finding the most outrageously naughty dishes to film in the Miami and Tallahassee areas. The phone began buzzing off the hook from restaurants all over Florida who wanted to hire me to take eye-catching images of their most creative and luxurious recipes. The Naughty Fork continued to steadily grow and became my full-time gig after graduating college. Filming through a lens of a city lifestyle met my personal experience of outrageous restaurant dining and really hit home with my growing online community. It was a life-changing moment for which I'm forever grateful. I had found my path.

With the ebb and flow of digital media also came content shifts for me, especially when restaurants closed during the pandemic. I quickly had to pivot my brand to bring the artful restaurant experience into the home by developing recipes. With my base of food knowledge, I taught myself to cook and set on a mission to share videos of delicious restaurant dishes that can be re-created easily. I found that I loved developing recipes and getting messy in the kitchen just as much as I loved showcasing chefs and restaurants.

After some time creating original recipes for my platform, sharing some of my iconic dishes as well as many new recipes through writing felt right. I can't wait for you to play with these recipes and flavors in your own home with friends and family. They are my true passion and inspiration, and the best definition of naughty.

NAUGHTY VS. NICE

Eating naughty is a vibe. I like to think of it as how we can turn a basic recipe up a few notches so that it becomes inherently impressive, decadent, and emotional to eat. That's how I want the recipes in this book to work for you. Forget bland meals. I've developed all of these flavors with the goal in mind of making sure cooking is approachable and easy, but so flavorful.

Eating naughty shouldn't be thought of as unhealthy. Yes, there are recipes that are more extravagant than others, but I strive to always cook in balance and moderation with high-quality ingredients to nourish the soul.

With that being said, some recipes can be elevated in certain ways that may add a more indulgent ingredient or two. To make sure you have multiple options of cooking a recipe that makes it adaptable to your lifestyle, I've included Nice versions of several Naughty recipes.

A Naughty recipe may have some added ingredients of richness to make them extra over the top in flavor. A Nice recipe may have some ingredients that are lighter in calories or are richer in nutrients for those days when you're trying to eat a little more whole. I'm all about moderation and balance; there are some days where I eat decadently 300 percent of the time, and other days where I look for heavy veg and lighter options.

I've designed this book with my audience in mind, so no matter what day of the week it is or season of the year, you'll know you're enjoying your food with naughty company.

THE NAUGHTY PANTRY

Even the most boring piece of bread becomes interesting with the right ingredients. Here's what I always keep in my pantry and fridge to elevate any meal to an emotional experience.

Salt

KOSHER: Keeping it real here, using this type of salt to season is GOLD. It's what restaurants use to enhance the flavor of every dish just right.

FLAKY SEA SALT: Required for ultimate naughtiness, use this to finish a recipe; it adds an extra crunch and heightens all flavors in each bite.

Oils

EXTRA-VIRGIN OLIVE OIL: The mother of oils. Use in salad dressings, stovetop, marinades, etc. Buy a high-quality brand and make sure it's 100 percent olive oil rather than an oil blend. You don't want to skimp on this.

AVOCADO OIL: My neutral oil of choice for high-heat cooking. I love to use it for shallow-frying and searing at high temperatures.

CALABRIAN CHILI OIL: Use this on EVERYTHING. It's basically my more bougie version of chili flakes.

SESAME OIL: You know, Asian cuisines are some of my top loves, and sesame oil is the foundation of much of that cooking.

COCONUT OIL: Great for baked goods; gives that hint of tropical flair.

Dairy

GREEK YOGURT: When it comes to Greek yogurt, I always have a container in my fridge. I often lead with full-fat for its extra richness in flavor and creamy texture. If I'm looking to lighten things up, my easy swap is using a low-fat Greek yogurt instead.

NONDAIRY YOGURT: Is great for salad dressings and marinades when you want a hint of creaminess. Coconut yogurt is definitely my favorite for its light texture and subtle sweetness.

BURRATA: The QUEEN of cheeses in my book. Add her to anything; break and schmear before serving.

FRESH MOZZARELLA: Not just any mozz, but the most pillowy, creamy mozz you will ever eat.

GRUYÈRE: Yup, the stinky cheese. It's ridiculously addicting. Keep it around for melts, noodles, and caramelized onions.

PARMESAN CHEESE: It's salty and cheesy all in one bite. I recommend having a container of finely grated as well as a block in your fridge to grate yourself. It's something I grab constantly and is the cherry on top for so many savory dishes.

BUTTER: Can you ever have enough?! Unsalted for most cooking, salted when you want an extra pinch of flavor.

MILK: I'm a lover of all types. Cow milk, almond milk, oat milk. I specify types in my recipes, but you can often substitute with your favorites.

HEAVY CREAM: Need I say more? It's the creamy factor we're all missing from life every single day. Round out a sauce, add richness to a sweet dessert, it's just too good.

Dry Goods

GARLIC: All the garlicky goodness, add this to everything. Whole bulbs are required for roasting to a jammy consistency. Prepeeled garlic is great for quick weeknight cooking.

ONIONS AND SHALLOTS: Onions are required; sweet, yellow, and red are my go-tos. Shallots are the onion's fancier cousin, with a hint of sweeter flavor and pizzazz.

PASTA: Gather all the noods, any shape you like. Pasta with ridges, like rigatoni or penne, is best to adhere to heavier sauces. Long noodles, like bucatini or spaghetti, are perfect for light sauces. A flatter noodle, like pappardelle or tagliatelle, works great to bind to those decadent ground or shredded meat sauces like a ragù.

FLOUR: All-purpose is my go-to. Occasionally, I use bread flour, which has more gluten than all-purpose, making the end product more chewy and dense. With baked goods, sometimes I like an almond or oat for a lighter texture and rich flavor (plus it's great for my gluten-free friends).

BUTTER CRACKERS: Aka one of the only crackers you need in your pantry. They're great for not just dipping but also for crushing to coat or top proteins, casseroles, salads—the list is endless.

The Sweet Stuff

GRANULATED SUGAR: Required mainly for baked goods, gives them their sweetness and texture.

BROWN SUGAR: I mean need I say more? It's just plain decadent. There's light and dark. I use dark for a deeper molasses flavor.

HONEY: One of my favorite ingredients for sweet and savory recipes. It just adds that little floral note.

MAPLE SYRUP: A little sweeter than honey with a bump of caramel-like flavor perfect for so many sweet treats.

AGAVE: I often sub this for granulated sugar in savory recipes. A little goes a long way; a drop gives any recipe just the right amount of sweetness, plus it's so easy to combine in sauces.

MORNING AFTER

When I'm having a night out, the ingredients for this Taco Bell–inspired breakfast crunch wrap are already in my fridge, waiting for me to get home. What else would you be doing at 2 a.m. besides making these? Whether I'm making them for my friends or as a party of one after a long night out, every bite is truly an irresistible journey of textures and flavors. From the fluffy scrambled eggs, to the crispy seasoned hash browns all cozied up between flour tortillas, nothing hits the spot better.

Seasoned Hash Browns

1 tablespoon chili powder

1½ teaspoons ground cumin

1 teaspoon garlic powder

Pinch of cayenne pepper

1 teaspoon kosher salt, plus more to taste

Freshly ground black pepper

3 tablespoons avocado oil, plus more as needed

1 pound frozen shredded hash brown potatoes

½ yellow onion, diced

Crunch Wraps

1½ tablespoons unsalted butter

12 large eggs, beaten

1½ cups grated yellow cheddar cheese

Kosher salt and freshly ground black pepper

4 burrito-size flour tortillas

12 ounces loose breakfast sausage, cooked and crumbled

Naughty Sauce (page 259)

1 cup grated pepper Jack cheese (4 ounces)

4 taco-size flour tortillas

1 tablespoon avocado oil, plus more as needed

PREP
25 minutes

COOK
45 minutes

MAKES
4 wraps

RECIPE
CONTINUES

Breakfast Crunch Wraps

- **Make the seasoned hash browns:** In a small bowl, combine the chili powder, cumin, garlic powder, cayenne, salt, and black pepper to taste. Set the spice blend aside.

- Line a plate with paper towels and have near the stove. In a large nonstick skillet, heat 2 tablespoons of the avocado oil over medium heat. Add half of the hash browns in an even layer and sprinkle with half of the onions and half the spice blend. Press the hash browns down gently with a spatula and allow to fry until golden brown and crispy, about 6 minutes.

- Flip the hash browns, adding the remaining 1 tablespoon oil around the rim of the pan. Cook until golden brown on the second side, another 5 to 6 minutes. Remove to the paper towels and sprinkle with salt. Repeat with the second half of the hash browns, onion, and spice blend and additional oil as needed.

- **Make the crunch wraps:** In the same nonstick skillet, melt the butter over medium-low heat. Add the eggs, sprinkle with ½ cup of the cheddar, and allow them to set for 30 seconds. Using a silicone spatula, begin gently pulling the outside edge of the eggs inward to form large soft curds. Continue stirring until the eggs are just cooked through, another 2 to 3 minutes. Season with salt and pepper to taste. Set aside, reserving the pan.

- On one burrito-size tortilla, place 1 cup of eggs in the center of the tortilla, leaving a 1½-inch border. Top with ¼ cup of the cheddar, ½ cup of the seasoned hash browns, ¼ cup of the sausage, 1½ tablespoons Naughty Sauce, and ¼ cup of the pepper Jack cheese. Place the taco-size tortilla on top and begin folding the sides inward to form a disc shape.

- Wipe out the same nonstick skillet and heat 1 tablespoon of the avocado oil over medium-low heat. Add the crunch wrap seam-side down and cook until golden brown on each side, 2 to 3 minutes per side. Remove to a plate and repeat with the remaining ingredients to make 4 crunch wraps total, adding more avocado oil as needed.

- Serve warm with additional Naughty Sauce on the side.

Make It Nice

Swap the breakfast sausage with loose chicken sausage. If you desire, you can use low-carb flour tortillas as well.

Candied bacon is like a secret weapon. You have the saltiness of regular delicious bacon that you dress up with a layer of brown sugar and a kick of cayenne pepper. It brings a new elegance to that sexy meat and pairs perfectly with the delicate layers of a flaky croissant. Naughty, indeed.

Candied Bacon

Cooking spray, for the rack

¼ cup (packed) light brown sugar

Pinch of cayenne pepper

Freshly ground black pepper

8 thick-cut slices bacon

Croissant Sandwiches

4 croissants

4 tablespoons (2 ounces/ ½ stick) unsalted butter; 2 tablespoons melted

6 large eggs, beaten

Kosher salt and freshly ground black pepper

½ cup grated white cheddar cheese

8 thin slices Black Forest ham (about 8 ounces)

½ cup grated Gruyère cheese

2 tablespoons chopped fresh chives

¼ cup honey mustard

PREP
15 minutes

COOK
50 minutes

MAKES
4 sandwiches

● **Make the candied bacon:** Preheat the oven to 300°F. Line a baking sheet with foil and top with a wire rack. Spritz the rack with cooking spray.

● In a medium bowl, combine the brown sugar, cayenne, and black pepper to taste. Dredge the pieces of bacon in the sugar mixture on both sides, shaking off any excess, and add the bacon to the wire rack.

● Bake until golden brown and crispy, 30 minutes. Remove from the oven, and increase the oven temperature to 400°F.

● Let cool on the rack for 10 minutes to continue crisping. Then remove the bacon strips to a plate to fully cool and crisp. Set aside.

● **Make the croissant sandwiches:** Line a baking sheet with parchment paper. In the now-400°F oven, add the croissants to the baking sheet and brush the tops with the 2 tablespoons melted butter. Toast in the oven until golden brown, about 3 minutes. Allow to cool slightly, then cut in half like a sandwich and place the bottoms back onto the baking sheet.

● Meanwhile, in a large nonstick skillet, heat the remaining 2 tablespoons butter over medium-low heat. Add the eggs and allow to set for 30 seconds. Using a silicone spatula, begin gently pulling the outside of the eggs inward to form large curds and season with salt and pepper to taste. Continue gently stirring until the eggs are just cooked and still fairly soft, another 2 to 3 minutes, adding the cheddar during the last minute of cooking.

RECIPE CONTINUES

Candied Bacon Croissant Breakfast Sandwiches

CANDIED BACON CROISSANT BREAKFAST SANDWICHES, CONTINUED

- To the bottom half of each croissant, add 2 slices ham, evenly top with the eggs, and sprinkle with the Gruyère. Place into the oven to melt the cheese, about 2 minutes.

- Remove from the oven and top with the chives and 2 slices candied bacon. Spread 1 tablespoon of the honey mustard on the inside of the top half of each croissant and place on the bottom. Enjoy warm!

- Store any leftovers eggs or bacon in separate airtight containers in the fridge. Wrap the croissants in plastic wrap and keep at room temperature. Keep for up to 1 day and reheat and assemble before serving.

This breakfast sandwich will make you and your friends pinch themselves—but you're not dreaming. Buttery brioche is slathered with any pesto you have on hand and topped with crispy prosciutto and not one, but two fried eggs for extra drippy decadence. Melted Swiss cheese holds this baby together for a rich bite that will linger on your tongue. It's a recipe great for breakfast or brunch, but one that I also wouldn't deny for lunch or dinner!

1 (4-ounce) package thinly sliced prosciutto

4 tablespoons (2 ounces/½ stick) unsalted butter, plus more as needed

4 large brioche buns, split

8 large eggs

Kosher salt and freshly ground black pepper

4 slices Swiss cheese

Basil Pistachio Pesto (page 261)

1 very ripe large tomato, thinly sliced

Sweet & Spicy Chili Crunch (optional; page 257), for garnish

1 avocado, thinly sliced

2 cups baby arugula

PREP
15 minutes

COOK
15 minutes

MAKES
4 sandwiches

● Preheat the oven to 400°F. Line a baking sheet with parchment paper.

● Evenly lay the prosciutto strips on the lined pan and bake, until deeper in color and crisp, 10 to 12 minutes. Set aside to cool completely (they will continue to crisp as they cool).

● In a large nonstick skillet, heat 2 tablespoons of the butter over medium-low heat. Add half of the buns cut-side down and allow to toast until golden brown, 1 to 2 minutes. Remove to a plate and repeat with the remaining buns, adding more butter as needed. Set aside.

● In the same skillet, add another 2 tablespoons butter. Carefully add the eggs, one by one, and cover the pan. Cook over medium-low heat until the whites are set but the yolk is still runny, 3 to 4 minutes. Season with salt and pepper to taste. During the last minute of cooking, top 4 of the eggs with a slice of Swiss cheese and return the lid to the pan to help the cheese melt.

● On the bottom of each brioche bun, spread 1 tablespoon of the pesto. Top with a slice of tomato, fried egg, then a second fried egg with the melted cheese. Add a drizzle of the chili crunch (if using), avocado slices, a hearty pinch of arugula, and 2 pieces of crispy prosciutto. Add the top bun and eat immediately. Serve with additional basil pistachio pesto on the side.

Make It Nice

Swap the brioche buns for a slice of sourdough toast to make an open-faced sandwich. Opt for crumbled feta cheese in place of the Swiss cheese.

● To serve, spread the 1 tablespoon pesto on each piece of toast. Top with the fried eggs, chili crunch (if using), and crumbled feta. Add a slice of tomato and hearty pinch of arugula and serve.

Pesto & Fried Egg Brioche Sandwiches

For a breakfast that's both naughty and nice, dive into this refreshing fruit bowl. With its jeweled decadence showcasing all my favorite fruits, it's the "Louis" of fruit bowls with its five-star finesse. Best to be spooned with only your finest silver.

Coconut Lime Dressing
Juice of 3 limes

1 tablespoon agave

⅓ cup coconut water

Fruit Salad
2 cups ½-inch cubes watermelon

1 cup ½-inch cubes cored fresh pineapple

1 cup ½-inch cubes cantaloupe

1 dragonfruit, peeled and cut into ½-inch cubes

½ mango, cut into ½-inch cubes (about ½ cup)

2 kiwifruits, peeled and cut into ½-inch cubes (about 1 cup)

½ cup blueberries

½ cup fresh raspberries

1 (0.75-ounce) bag freeze-dried raspberries or strawberries

2 tablespoons chopped fresh mint

¼ cup mini chocolate chips

½ cup your favorite granola

PREP
25 minutes

SERVES
6

● **Make the coconut lime dressing:** In a small bowl, whisk together the lime juice, agave, and coconut water.

● **Make the fruit salad:** In a large bowl, combine the watermelon, pineapple, cantaloupe, dragonfruit, mango, kiwifruits, blueberries, and fresh raspberries. Drizzle with the coconut lime dressing and toss gently to combine.

● Add the freeze-dried raspberries right before serving and toss again. Garnish with mint, mini chocolate chips, and granola.

The Whole Fruit Bowl Salad

Candy bars for breakfast? I'd call it a naughty way to start the day. These protein bites remind me of a Reese's Peanut Butter Cup and are highly addictive, but they have a healthy twist with protein powder. A crunchy dark chocolate outer layer coats the melt-in-your-mouth peanut butter center that's also high in protein. These are perfectly poppable, chewy, and rich—I can already advise to keep a batch in your freezer at all times.

2 cups old-fashioned rolled oats

1 cup pitted Medjool dates, roughly chopped

1 cup all-natural creamy peanut butter

⅓ cup honey

1 scoop vanilla protein powder

2 to 4 tablespoons warm water

½ cup salted roasted peanuts

1 cup dark chocolate chips (8 ounces)

1 tablespoon coconut oil

PREP
25 minutes

COOK
3 minutes

MAKES
36 balls

- Line a baking sheet with parchment paper and set aside.

- In a food processor, blend the oats until a fine flour texture forms. Add the dates, peanut butter, honey, and protein powder and blend until a smooth dough forms, stirring every so often, 1 to 2 minutes.

- Add a couple tablespoons warm water as needed depending on how moist the dates are. Blend again until the dough comes together.

- Add ⅓ cup of the peanuts and pulse one last time until the peanuts are roughly chopped in the filling.

- Using a 1-ounce cookie scoop (or 2 tablespoons using a tablespoon measure), scoop the dough onto the baking sheet and roll to make a smooth ball.

- In a microwave-safe medium bowl, combine the chocolate chips and coconut oil. Microwave in 30-second intervals, stirring after each, until the chocolate mixture is melted and very smooth.

- Dip the balls into the chocolate mixture, allowing any excess chocolate to drip off, and return to the baking sheet.

- Roughly chop the remaining peanuts and sprinkle over the top to garnish. Refrigerate the balls for 15 minutes until the chocolate is set. These are best stored in the freezer for up to 1 month.

Make It Nice

An alternative version for almond lovers is to substitute almond flour for the oat flour. Swap almond butter for the peanut butter, and salted roasted almonds for the peanuts. Lastly, use unsweetened (no sugar added) dark chocolate chips instead of dark chocolate chips.

Peanut Butter Crunch Protein Bites

Silky and sultry: That's the only way to describe these eggs. The recipe features poached eggs over a bed of pillowy Greek yogurt dripping in Aleppo pepper–infused butter. My twist turns this into a toast, with a piece of thick crusty bread to sop up all the flavors into one droolworthy bite.

Poached Eggs

2 teaspoons distilled white vinegar

2 large eggs

Aleppo Pepper Sauce

4 tablespoons (2 ounces/ ½ stick) unsalted butter

¼ cup extra-virgin olive oil

1 teaspoon Aleppo pepper

¼ teaspoon kosher salt

Freshly ground black pepper

Yogurt Toast

4 tablespoons extra-virgin olive oil

4 slices (1 inch thick) sourdough bread

2 cups whole-milk Greek yogurt

Grated zest of 1 lemon

Juice of ½ lemon

2 garlic cloves, grated

½ teaspoon ground cumin

¼ teaspoon smoked paprika

½ teaspoon kosher salt, plus more to taste

For Serving

1 tablespoon chopped fresh dill

Aleppo pepper

Flaky sea salt

Lemon wedges, for squeezing

PREP
25 minutes

COOK
10 minutes

SERVES
2

● **Poach the eggs:** Line a plate with paper towels and have near the stove. Bring a medium saucepan of water to a simmer over medium-low heat. Add the vinegar and stir to combine.

● Crack the eggs one at a time into individual ramekins. Stir the water in a circular direction to create a whirlpool effect. Add the eggs, one by one, occasionally stirring to keep a gentle circular motion. Cook until the whites are cooked but the yolk is still runny, 3 to 4 minutes. Using a slotted spoon, remove the eggs carefully to the paper towels to drain. Set aside.

● **Make the Aleppo pepper sauce:** In a small saucepan, heat the butter and olive oil over medium-low heat until the butter melts. Add the Aleppo pepper and swirl to infuse the flavor. Season with the salt and black pepper to taste.

● **Make the yogurt toast:** In a large skillet, heat 2 tablespoons of the olive oil over medium-low heat. Add 2 slices of bread and toast on both sides until golden brown, about 2 minutes per side. Remove to a plate. Repeat with the remaining 2 tablespoons olive oil and bread slices.

Turkish Egg & Garlicky Yogurt Toast

● In a food processor, combine the yogurt, lemon zest, lemon juice, garlic, cumin, and smoked paprika and pulse until light and fluffy. Season with the salt. Remove the yogurt to a piping bag or zip-top bag and cut off the tip to make about a ¾-inch opening.

● Pipe the whipped Greek yogurt on top of each piece of toast in a zigzag pattern. Place each piece of olive oil toast on a shallow bowl or rimmed plate and top with a poached egg. Drizzle with the Aleppo pepper sauce. Sprinkle over fresh dill, more Aleppo pepper, and flaky sea salt and serve with a squeeze of lemon.

Make It Nice

Swap the whole-milk Greek yogurt for 0% or 2%. Omit the butter in the Aleppo pepper sauce and add a tablespoon of olive oil, to make 5 tablespoons in total.

● To serve, schmear the whipped Greek yogurt on the bottom of a shallow bowl. Top with the poached eggs and a drizzle of the Aleppo-infused olive oil. Serve with half a piece of sourdough toast.

Turkish Egg & Garlicky Yogurt Toast, page 34

It's a bacon-egg-and-cheese on the go. It's poppable and also super cute. Everything you need for breakfast in one bite. Line a muffin tin with flaky, buttery puff pastry, then top with a rich filling of soft-cooked eggs and smoky bacon for a layered mouthful that starts any day off right.

6 slices bacon

Cooking spray, for greasing

8 large eggs, beaten

¼ cup heavy cream

1 teaspoon kosher salt

Freshly ground black pepper

All-purpose flour, for dusting

1 (17.3-ounce) package frozen puff pastry, thawed

2 tablespoons Dijon mustard

1 cup grated yellow cheddar cheese

1 tablespoon everything bagel seasoning

2 tablespoons minced fresh chives, for garnish

Naughty Sauce (page 259), for serving

PREP
25 minutes

COOK
40 minutes

MAKES
12 cups

● Line a plate with paper towels and have near the stove. Line a baking sheet with foil and evenly lay out the bacon strips. Place into a cold oven and turn the oven to 400°F. Allow to cook, flipping halfway through, until deeply browned and crisp, 18 to 22 minutes.

● Remove the bacon from the oven and place on the paper towels to cool and crisp. Once cooled, cut the strips in half.

● Keep the oven temperature at 400°F and grease 12 cups of a muffin tin with cooking spray.

● In a large bowl, combine the eggs, heavy cream, and salt and pepper to taste. Whisk well until smooth. Set aside.

● On a lightly floured surface, roll out the first sheet of puff pastry to a 12 × 8-inch rectangle. Cut the puff pastry into six 4-inch squares. Place the 6 squares into the bottom of 6 muffin cups as the base. Repeat with the second piece of puff pastry to fill the remaining 6 cups of the muffin tin.

● Add one piece of bacon to the bottom of each cup and top with a little schmear of mustard. Evenly divide ½ cup of the cheddar among the muffin cups.

● Ladle the egg mixture into each cup and evenly top with the remaining ½ cup cheddar. Sprinkle with the everything bagel seasoning and transfer to the oven.

● Bake until the puff pastry is golden brown and the eggs are cooked through, 16 to 18 minutes.

● Garnish with the chives and serve hot with Naughty Sauce on the side.

● To store, simply cool to room temperature and then place in an airtight container or bag to freeze for up to 2 months. Reheat in a 350°F oven for 8 to 12 minutes until warmed through.

Puff Pastry BEC Cups

There's something I can't resist about a recipe that plays nice but tastes naughty. And these strawberry shortcake baked oats may be the quintessential example—think of them as a breakfast cobbler of sorts. They're sweet and tart and give that "lick the bottom of the bowl" energy every time. Plus baking them in small ramekins to make individual servings truly elevates oatmeal into an elegant hotel-style brunch dish that's easy to serve to a crowd. I love this strawberry version, but you can really use any fresh berries or fruit you like.

1 tablespoon unsalted butter, for the ramekins

2 cups old-fashioned rolled oats

1 teaspoon baking powder

1 teaspoon ground cinnamon

½ teaspoon kosher salt

1¼ cups whole milk

2 large eggs

⅓ cup honey

1 teaspoon pure vanilla extract

6 ounces strawberries, hulled and sliced (about 1¼ cups)

For Serving

½ cup cold heavy cream

4 ounces cream cheese, at room temperature (½ cup)

1 tablespoon honey

3 ounces strawberries, hulled and sliced (about ½ cup), for garnish

2 tablespoons finely crushed freeze-dried strawberries, for garnish

PREP
15 minutes

COOK
30 minutes

SERVES
6

• Preheat the oven to 375°F. Grease six 4-ounce ramekins with the butter.

• In a large bowl, stir together the oats, baking powder, cinnamon, and salt.

• In a medium bowl, whisk together the milk, eggs, honey, and vanilla. Make a well in the center of the dry ingredients and pour the milk mixture in the center. Gently fold everything together to combine.

• Add the strawberries and fold gently again to incorporate. Divide the oat mixture evenly among the ramekins and place them on a baking sheet.

• Bake until the tops are golden brown and the center has set, 25 to 30 minutes.

• Let cool for 10 minutes before serving.

• **To serve:** In a medium bowl, with an electric mixer, beat the heavy cream on medium speed until stiff peaks form, 3 to 4 minutes. Gently fold in the cream cheese and honey until smooth and combined.

• Dollop the whipped cream cheese on top of each ramekin. Garnish with sliced strawberries and a sprinkle of freeze-dried strawberries.

• To store, let cool to room temperature and wrap in plastic to cover. Refrigerate for up to 4 days. Reheat in the microwave for a couple of minutes until warmed through.

Make It Nice

Substitute whipped Greek yogurt for the whipped cream and cream cheese: In a medium bowl, with an electric mixer, beat 1 cup 2% Greek yogurt and 1 tablespoon honey on medium speed until light and fluffy, about 2 minutes. Spoon on top of the baked oats to garnish.

Strawberry Shortcake Baked Oats

Your egg game is about to be transformed in a naughty way; behold the chili crisp egg. Start by throwing homemade chili crisp into a skillet to fry eggs to sunny-side-up perfection. Cradle them in a tortilla with your favorite toppings, and I guarantee you'll be seduced by eggs in a way you never thought possible.

1 tablespoon extra-virgin olive oil

½ cup grated cheddar cheese

2 tablespoons Sweet & Spicy Chili Crunch (page 257)

4 large eggs

4 taco-size flour tortillas, warmed

1 avocado, thinly sliced

½ cup Too Easy Pickled Radishes (page 265)

1 teaspoon toasted sesame seeds

¼ cup packed fresh cilantro leaves, for garnish

¼ cup sliced scallions, for garnish

PREP
5 minutes

COOK
5 minutes

MAKES
4 tacos
(Serves 2)

● In a large nonstick skillet, combine the olive oil, cheddar, and chili crunch over medium-low heat. Once sizzling, crack the eggs around the pan. Cover the pan and cook until the whites are opaque but the yolk is still runny, 4 to 6 minutes.

● Place one egg onto each warmed tortilla and top with avocado slices, pickled radishes, sesame seeds, cilantro, and scallions. Serve immediately.

Chili Crisp Breakfast Tacos

My friends are huge fans of these. They're easy to make and great for a last-minute brunch. There are so many different flavor combinations to try, but I love this Monte Cristo–inspired version with ham, egg, cheddar, and blackberry jam for a savory-sweet combo that's truly delightful.

5 tablespoons unsalted butter

8 large eggs, beaten

1 teaspoon kosher salt, plus more to taste

Freshly ground black pepper

1 teaspoon fresh thyme

1 (12-ounce) package Hawaiian slider rolls (12 rolls)

2 tablespoons Dijon mustard

¾ pound thick-sliced ham or thinly sliced Black Forest ham

6 slices yellow cheddar cheese

½ cup blackberry jam

1 tablespoon honey

Flaky sea salt

Powdered sugar (optional), for garnish

PREP
15 minutes

COOK
14 minutes

SERVES
6 to 8

- In a large nonstick skillet, heat 3 tablespoons of the butter over medium-low heat. Add the eggs, season with the salt, and allow to set for 30 seconds. Using a silicone spatula, gently pull the outer edge of the eggs inward to form large curds. Continue gently stirring until the eggs are soft and just cooked through, about 2 minutes. Season with more salt and pepper to taste and set aside.

- Preheat the oven to 375°F. Line a baking sheet with parchment paper.

- In a small saucepan, melt the remaining 2 tablespoons butter over medium-low heat. Stir in the thyme and season with a pinch of salt. Remove from the heat and set aside.

- Split the Hawaiian slider rolls open, making sure the rolls stay attached on one side. Evenly spread the mustard over the bottom layer of buns. Top with sliced ham, scrambled eggs, and slices of cheddar. Dollop the blackberry jam over the top of the cheese and drizzle lightly with honey.

- Place the top bun over the top of everything. Set the buns on the lined baking sheet. Brush the tops of the buns with the melted thyme butter and sprinkle with flaky sea salt.

- Bake until the cheese has melted and the tops of the buns are golden, 8 to 10 minutes.

- Allow the sandwiches to cool for 5 minutes, then slice and serve. Dust with powdered sugar as desired.

Blackberry Monte Cristo Breakfast Sliders

YOU'RE A SNACK

Let's just take a moment to imagine hopping onto a boat on the Amalfi Coast to have lunch. It's a beautiful day, and you sit down to a glass of rosé and thin, crisp, dainty breadsticks wrapped with prosciutto. Now, imagine you're back in the United States, coming home from a night out to a package of frozen breadsticks—the starchy variety, not the delicate grissini you had in Italy. My version is the ultimate trifecta of garlicky cheese, prosciutto, and bread. Sometimes I just drape the prosciutto on top of the breadstick before baking, to make these even simpler, but you can also wrap it around to get a more lollipop effect.

- Preheat the oven to 375°F. Line a baking sheet with parchment paper.

- Place the breadsticks onto the lined baking sheet. Brush each breadstick with the herb and garlic cheese spread and sprinkle with the cayenne. Wrap the prosciutto around each breadstick.

- Bake until the breadsticks are golden brown and the prosciutto is lightly crispy, about 18 minutes.

- Sprinkle with the Parmesan and Italian seasoning. Serve with marinara sauce for dipping.

1 (10-ounce) package frozen garlic breadsticks (about 6 per package)

½ (5.3-ounce) package garlic and herb cheese spread (I like Boursin), warmed

¼ teaspoon cayenne pepper

1 (4-ounce) package thinly sliced prosciutto

2 tablespoons freshly grated Parmesan cheese

1 teaspoon Italian seasoning

Marinara sauce, warmed, for dipping

PREP
10 minutes

COOK
12 minutes

SERVES
6

Not Your Nonna's Italian Lollipops

Want to know what my secret weapon ingredient is? Puff pastry. It puts the glam in any drab app or side dish. Those flaky layers are oh so buttery and crunchy with each bite. And with pizza? It's a love affair that just makes sense. This is my pepperoni version, and my naughty tip is to crisp the pepperoni in the oven before stuffing inside the turnover for extra texture. It elevates the cheese and marinara sauce to a gooey bite that's difficult to deny.

1 (4-ounce) package pepperoni slices

1 cup marinara sauce

2 teaspoons Italian seasoning

4 garlic cloves, grated

Kosher salt and freshly ground black pepper

All-purpose flour, for dusting

1 (17.3-ounce) package frozen puff pastry, thawed

1 cup freshly grated whole-milk mozzarella (about 4 ounces)

1 large egg, beaten

¼ cup freshly grated Parmesan cheese, plus more for garnish

Pinch of dried oregano, for garnish

¼ cup hot honey, for garnish

PREP
20 minutes

COOK
58 minutes

MAKES
8 turnovers

- Preheat the oven to 400°F. Line three baking sheets with parchment paper.

- Lay the pepperoni slices on one of the prepared baking sheets. Bake until the pepperoni slices have crisped, 6 to 8 minutes. Remove from the oven and allow to cool. Roughly chop.

- In a small bowl, stir together the marinara sauce, Italian seasoning, garlic, and salt and pepper to taste.

- Lightly dust the counter with flour. Using a rolling pin, roll one piece of puff pastry into a 12-inch square. Cut into 4 squares.

- Spread the marinara sauce onto each piece of puff pastry, leaving a ½-inch border. Top with 2 tablespoons mozzarella and 1 tablespoon pepperoni.

- Brush the beaten egg around the edge of the puff pastry and fold into a triangle. Using the tines of a fork, press the edges to seal. Cut a small slit in the top to release steam for each turnover and place on the second prepared baking sheet.

- Repeat with the remaining sheet of puff pastry and filling ingredients to make 8 turnovers total. Brush the tops of the turnovers with egg and sprinkle with the Parmesan.

- Bake one baking sheet of turnovers at a time on the center rack of the oven until the puff pastry is golden brown and flaky, about 25 minutes per baking sheet.

- Sprinkle with additional Parmesan cheese and dried oregano, and drizzle with hot honey. Serve.

- To store any leftovers, simply wrap them well in plastic wrap or foil and keep in the fridge for up to 1 day. Reheat in an oven preheated to 350°F or a toaster oven, for 5 to 10 minutes, until warmed through and crispy.

Pizza Turnovers

Step aside, avocado toast, this pesto Caprese toast will transform your toast game. Schmear a thick layer of my basil pistachio pesto on top of golden-brown bread, topped with juicy heirloom tomatoes, and the queen of cheese, burrata. If you're feeling extra naughty, some prosciutto wouldn't hurt.

4 tablespoons extra-virgin olive oil

4 slices (¾ inch thick) sourdough bread

1 large garlic clove

1 cup Basil Pistachio Pesto (page 261)

1 (3-ounce) package prosciutto slices (optional)

1 large ripe heirloom tomato, thinly sliced

4 (2-ounce) mini balls burrata

Garnishes
Flaky sea salt

Fresh basil leaves, torn

Red chile flakes

Balsamic reduction

PREP
10 minutes

COOK
10 minutes

SERVES
4

● In a large skillet, heat 2 tablespoons of the olive oil over medium heat. Once it's shimmering, add 2 pieces of bread and toast until golden brown, 2 to 3 minutes per side. Repeat with the remaining olive oil and bread. Once toasted, rub the garlic clove on the top side of each piece of bread to add a kiss of flavor.

● Spread 2 to 3 tablespoons of pesto on top of each toast. Top each toast with slices of prosciutto (if using), tomato slices, and 1 burrata ball.

● When ready to serve, cut the burrata open and garnish with flaky sea salt, basil leaves, chile flakes, and a drizzle of balsamic reduction.

Pesto Caprese Toast

Hot honey may be the ultimate tease of all the condiments for me. It adds the special little finishing touch on pizza, toast, veggies, and of course hot fried chicken. These crispy chicken bites are alllll the things: spicy, sweet, crunchy, juicy, and moist. Truly a nugget that'll keep you longing for more.

Hot Honey Sauce

¾ cup honey

2 tablespoons red chile flakes

1 tablespoon fresh lemon juice

Crispy Chicken Bites

Canola oil, for deep-frying

1 pound boneless, skinless chicken breasts (2 to 3), cut into 1-inch pieces

Kosher salt and freshly ground black pepper

1 cup all-purpose flour

2 teaspoons paprika

2 teaspoons garlic powder

2 teaspoons onion powder

3 large eggs, beaten

1¼ cups crushed cornflakes

1½ cups panko bread crumbs

2 tablespoons chopped fresh chives, for garnish

PREP
20 minutes

COOK
20 minutes

SERVES
4 to 6

● **Make the hot honey sauce:** In a small saucepan, heat the honey and chile flakes over medium-low heat until the honey smells spicy, 3 to 5 minutes. Remove from the heat and stir in the lemon juice. Place a fine-mesh sieve over a bowl. Strain the hot honey through the sieve to remove the chile flakes. Set aside and keep warm.

● **Make the crispy chicken bites:** Set a wire rack in a sheet pan and have near the stove. Pour 3 inches of canola oil into a large Dutch oven or heavy-bottomed pot and heat over medium-high heat to 360°F on a deep-frying thermometer.

● Season the chicken pieces with salt and pepper.

● **Set up a dredging station with three shallow bowls:** In the first bowl, whisk the flour, paprika, garlic powder, and onion powder to combine. In the second bowl, beat the eggs. In the third bowl, add the cornflakes and panko and mix to combine. Season each bowl well with salt and pepper.

● Dredge the chicken pieces in flour, dip in the egg, and dredge in the cornflake/panko mixture, shaking off any excess with each step. Working in batches to avoid overcrowding, place the chicken in the hot oil and fry until golden brown and the chicken is cooked to 165°F on a meat thermometer, 4 to 6 minutes. Drain the chicken on a wire rack and season with salt.

● Once all the chicken is fried, place in a large bowl and drizzle with the hot honey sauce. Toss to lightly coat. Garnish with chives and serve immediately.

Make It Nice

Bake the chicken instead of frying. Preheat the oven to 425°F. Place a wire rack in a sheet pan. Add the dredged chicken pieces to the rack and lightly spray with cooking spray. Bake until golden brown and the chicken registers 165°F on a meat thermometer, 16 to 18 minutes. Toss in the hot honey sauce and garnish with chives.

Hot Honey Crispy Chicken Bites

You heard it right, it's Bang Bang Shrimp, the appetizer that truly speaks for itself. Crunchy fried shrimp are coated in a creamy, sweet, and spicy Thai chili sauce that's sure to win anyone over. It's the ideal app to start off a spicy evening, if you catch my drift.

Sweet Chili Sauce

½ cup mayonnaise

⅓ cup Thai sweet chili sauce

2 teaspoons sriracha

2 tablespoons rice vinegar

½ teaspoon kosher salt

Fried Shrimp

Canola oil, for deep-frying

1 cup all-purpose flour

¾ cup low-fat buttermilk, shaken

⅓ cup cornstarch

1 teaspoon sriracha

1 teaspoon paprika

1½ teaspoons garlic powder

1 teaspoon onion powder

2 cups panko bread crumbs

Kosher salt and freshly ground black pepper

1 pound peeled and deveined large shrimp

3 scallions (green parts only), thinly sliced, for garnish

PREP
15 minutes

COOK
15 minutes

SERVES
4 to 6

● **Make the sweet chili sauce:** In a medium bowl, whisk together the mayonnaise, Thai sweet chili sauce, sriracha, vinegar, and salt. Set aside.

● **Make the fried shrimp:** Set a wire rack in a sheet pan and have near the stove. Pour 2 inches of canola oil into a large Dutch oven or heavy-bottomed pot and heat over medium-high heat to 325°F on a deep-frying thermometer.

● **Set up a dredging station with three shallow bowls:** In the first bowl, add the flour. In the second bowl, add the buttermilk, cornstarch, sriracha, paprika, garlic powder, and onion powder and whisk to combine. In the third bowl, add the panko. Season each bowl well with salt and pepper.

● Season the shrimp with salt. Dredge half of the shrimp in the flour, then dip in the buttermilk mixture, and finally coat in the panko, shaking off any excess. Fry the shrimp until lightly golden and cooked through, 3 to 4 minutes. Remove to the wire rack and season with salt. Repeat with the remaining shrimp.

● In a large bowl, combine the shrimp and half of the sauce. Toss to lightly coat the shrimp, adding more sauce as desired. Garnish with scallion greens and serve.

Bang Bang Shrimp

This is an appetizer that feels like a summer romance: bright, playful, and a harmony of flavors that will make you want to dance off into the sunset. The bread is fried in olive oil, smothered with pillowy ricotta, and topped with sweet caramelized peaches. It's one of those elegant apps everyone will ask how to make.

2 tablespoons extra-virgin olive oil, plus more as needed and for garnish

½ baguette, thinly sliced

2 tablespoons unsalted butter

2 peaches, chopped, or 1 (10-ounce) bag frozen peach slices, thawed and chopped

2 tablespoons light brown sugar

1 teaspoon fresh lemon juice

1 cup ricotta cheese

¼ cup baby arugula

Balsamic reduction, for garnish

Flaky sea salt, for garnish

PREP
15 minutes

COOK
15 minutes

SERVES
4 to 6

● In a large skillet, heat the olive oil over medium-low heat. Toast a couple slices of bread at a time until golden brown, 2 to 3 minutes. Remove to a plate and repeat with the remaining slices of bread, adding more olive oil as needed.

● In the same pan, heat the butter over medium-low heat. Add the peaches and brown sugar and cook until softened and lightly caramelized, 3 to 4 minutes. Add the lemon juice right as they finish cooking.

● Schmear some of the ricotta onto each slice of toast, using a table knife to cover. Spoon over the peaches and top with the arugula, a drizzle of olive oil and balsamic reduction, and a sprinkle of flaky sea salt.

Ricotta & Peach Toasts

Say hello to the deviled egg's naughty side. These are deep-fried and oh-so-sinful when compared to the classic. The creamy yolk filling is smooth and sultry as can be with a hint of spicy, thanks to pickled jalapeños. Topped with a hint of bacon, it's one insane flavor explosion.

15 large eggs

1 cup mayonnaise

1 tablespoon Dijon mustard

¼ teaspoon kosher salt, plus more to taste

¼ teaspoon freshly ground black pepper, plus more to taste

1 small garlic clove, grated

2 teaspoons chopped pickled jalapeños

Pinch of cayenne pepper

Grated zest of 1 lemon

Canola oil, for deep-frying

1½ cups all-purpose flour

1½ cups panko bread crumbs

⅓ cup finely grated Parmesan cheese

For Garnish

2 tablespoons ½-inch pieces fresh chives

2 slices bacon, cooked and chopped

Paprika

PREP
25 minutes

COOK
15 minutes

MAKES
24 deviled eggs

● Fill a large saucepan with water and bring to a boil over high heat. Add 12 of the eggs, reduce the heat to medium, and boil for 10 minutes. Drain, and when they are cool enough to handle, peel the eggs.

● Slice each egg in half lengthwise. Arrange the whites on a plate lined with paper towels and set aside. Transfer the yolks to a food processor and add the mayonnaise, mustard, salt, pepper, garlic, jalapeños, cayenne, and lemon zest. Process until well blended and smooth, scraping down the sides as necessary.

● Transfer the mixture to a resealable plastic bag. Seal the bag and place in the fridge while you fry the egg whites.

● Line a plate with paper towels and set near the stove. Pour 3 inches canola oil into a large Dutch oven or heavy-bottomed pot, and heat over medium-high heat to 350°F on a deep-frying thermometer.

● **Set up a dredging station with three shallow bowls:** In the first bowl, add the flour. In the second bowl, add the remaining 3 eggs and beat them. In the third bowl, combine the panko and Parmesan and mix to combine. Season each bowl well with salt and pepper.

● Pat the egg whites dry and then dredge in the flour, dusting off any excess. Dip into the beaten eggs and then evenly coat in the panko/Parmesan mixture.

● Working in batches to avoid overcrowding, place the egg whites in the hot oil and fry until golden brown on all sides, 3 to 4 minutes. Using a slotted spoon, remove the egg whites from the oil and drain on the paper towels.

● Cut off the end of the yolk filling bag using a pair of scissors. Pipe the filling into each egg half. Garnish with a sprinkling of chives, some bacon, and a light dusting of paprika.

Crispy Deviled Eggs

I mean, what slaps more than a massive cheeseball in the center of your table, especially one that's jalapeño popper–flavored? Cream cheese is studded with jalapeños, bacon, scallions, and spices and then rolled in jewels of fried onions for a cheesy disco ball of pure pleasure.

2 (8-ounce) blocks cream cheese, at room temperature

2 teaspoons garlic powder

1 teaspoon onion powder

½ teaspoon paprika

¼ teaspoon cayenne pepper

1 tablespoon honey

2 teaspoons kosher salt

¼ teaspoon freshly ground black pepper

1 pound bacon, cooked and finely crumbled

2 cups grated sharp yellow cheddar cheese

¼ cup finely chopped seeded fresh jalapeños (2 or 3)

1 bunch of scallions, chopped (about 1 cup)

½ cup store-bought fried onions, large pieces lightly crushed

For Serving
Butter crackers

Celery sticks

Carrot sticks

Sliced radishes

Hot sauce

PREP
25 minutes, plus 3 hours chilling

SERVES
8

- In a large bowl, using an electric mixer, combine the cream cheese, garlic powder, onion powder, paprika, cayenne, honey, salt, and black pepper and beat on medium speed until light and fluffy, 2 to 3 minutes.

- Stir in three-quarters each of the bacon crumbles, cheddar, jalapeños, and scallions and gently fold to combine. Set aside. Store the remaining ingredients in separate containers in the fridge until ready to serve.

- Line the countertop with two large pieces of plastic wrap. Place the cream cheese mixture in the center into a mound to begin making a ball shape. Grab the pieces of the plastic wrap up over the cream cheese mixture to help with forming a ball.

- Place the ball on a plate and refrigerate until the mixture is firm and set, at least 3 hours and up to overnight.

- When ready to serve, combine the remaining reserved bacon crumbles, cheddar, jalapeños, and scallions with the fried onions on a large rimmed plate or baking sheet.

- Unwrap the cheeseball and roll in the toppings to evenly cover all sides.

- **To serve:** Set the cheese ball on a platter and serve with butter crackers, celery and carrot sticks, radishes, and hot sauce for additional spice.

- Any cheeseball leftovers can be stored in the fridge covered with plastic wrap for up to 5 days.

Honey Jalapeño Popper Cheese Ball

When it comes to appetizer meatballs, they can often be bland. But not these—they're juicy and tender, ready to welcome the party dressed in a sweet and tangy sauce that's loaded with garlic. Add a dash of sesame and toothpicks and they'll disappear quickly before your eyes. A hot tip: They make a great main course, too, served over rice with roasted broccoli.

Chicken Meatballs

1 pound ground chicken

4 garlic cloves, grated

2 tablespoons chopped scallions, plus additional sliced (green parts only) for garnish

1 (1-inch) piece fresh ginger, peeled and chopped

½ cup panko bread crumbs

½ teaspoon red chile flakes

1 teaspoon kosher salt

Freshly ground black pepper

2 tablespoons avocado or canola oil

Sticky Honey Garlic Sauce

¼ cup reduced-sodium soy sauce

⅓ cup honey

3 garlic cloves, grated

2 tablespoons rice vinegar

1 teaspoon cornstarch

1 tablespoon sesame seeds, for garnish

PREP
20 minutes

COOK
20 minutes

SERVES
6 to 8

Make the chicken meatballs: In a large bowl, combine the chicken, garlic, scallions, ginger, panko, and chile flakes. Season with the salt and black pepper to taste and mix to combine.

Scoop the chicken mixture into 2-tablespoon amounts and roll into meatballs (you will have 15 to 18 meatballs). Chill the meatballs in the freezer for 10 minutes, if desired, to help them hold their shape when cooking.

In a large heavy-bottomed skillet, heat the oil over medium-high heat. Add the meatballs and sear on all sides until golden brown and 165°F on a meat thermometer, 10 to 12 minutes total. Remove the meatballs to a plate and set aside.

Make the sticky honey garlic sauce: Drain the skillet of any excess oil. Return the skillet to medium heat and deglaze the pan with ¼ cup water, scraping the browned bits up off the bottom. Add the soy sauce, honey, garlic, and vinegar. Bring to a boil, then reduce to a simmer and cook until reduced by a third and slightly thickened, about 3 minutes.

In a small bowl, stir together the cornstarch and 1 teaspoon water. Pour into the sauce and simmer again for a minute or so until thickened and the sauce coats the back of a spoon nicely.

Return the meatballs to the skillet and stir to coat in the sauce. Garnish with scallion greens and sesame seeds and serve with toothpicks.

Make It Nice

Rather than searing the meatballs, bake them on a parchment-lined baking sheet. Preheat the oven to 400°F and bake until the meatballs are 165°F on a meat thermometer and golden brown, 16 to 20 minutes.

Sticky Honey Garlic Meatballs

These are just adorable. It's as if sweet crunchy peppers had a love child with a taco. These babies are bursting with flavor and go well paired with any sauce, especially Naughty Sauce.

4 bell peppers, quartered lengthwise and seeded

2 tablespoons extra-virgin olive oil

½ pound ground beef (85/15)

½ yellow onion, diced

2 garlic cloves, minced

2 tablespoons chili powder

2 teaspoons ground cumin

¼ teaspoon ground cinnamon

Pinch of cayenne pepper

½ (15.5-ounce) can black beans, drained and rinsed

1 teaspoon kosher salt, plus more to taste

Freshly ground black pepper

1 cup grated yellow cheddar cheese

2 tablespoons chopped fresh cilantro

Naughty Sauce (page 259)

PREP
15 minutes

COOK
32 minutes

SERVES
6

• Preheat the oven to 400°F. Line a baking sheet with parchment paper.

• Place the quartered peppers on the baking sheet and roast until lightly tender, 7 to 9 minutes. Remove and set the baking sheet aside. Leave the oven on.

• Meanwhile, in a large skillet, heat the olive oil over medium heat. Add the beef, breaking it up with the back of a wooden spoon, and cook until browned, about 6 minutes. Add the onion and garlic and cook until softened, another 4 to 5 minutes.

• Add the chili powder, cumin, cinnamon, cayenne, black beans, salt, and black pepper to taste. Stir to combine and toast the spices, about a minute. Deglaze with ¼ cup water, scraping any browned bits off of the bottom of the pan, and simmer until the water has almost all evaporated.

• Evenly fill the quartered peppers with the ground beef mixture. Return to the oven and bake until the peppers are almost soft but still easy enough to pick up, 6 to 7 minutes.

• Remove from the oven and sprinkle with the cheddar. Return to the oven to melt the cheese, another 3 minutes. Garnish with cilantro and serve with Naughty Sauce.

Make It Nice

Swap out the ground beef for ground chicken or turkey. Top the peppers with only ½ cup cheese for melting.

Taco-Stuffed Pepper Bites

Crab rangoon is required anytime I order from my local Chinese takeout spot. It hits every craving—crunchy, creamy, sweet, salty, and spicy. These crab rangoon mozzarella sticks are an even more lavish, addicting version of the classic. You may want to hide some extras for yourself to enjoy in full privacy—they disappear in a crowd in the blink of an eye.

1 (8-ounce) package cream cheese, at room temperature

2 cups grated mozzarella cheese

8 ounces jumbo lump crabmeat, picked through for shells

¼ cup chopped scallions

1 tablespoon agave

1 teaspoon garlic powder

Pinch of cayenne pepper

1 tablespoon reduced-sodium soy sauce or tamari

1 tablespoon Worcestershire sauce

½ teaspoon kosher salt, plus more to taste

Canola oil, for frying

¾ cup all-purpose flour

3 large eggs, beaten

2 cups panko bread crumbs

Thai sweet chili sauce, for serving

PREP
25 minutes, plus freezing time

COOK
10 minutes

MAKES
16 mozzarella sticks

- Line an 8 × 8-inch baking dish with two pieces of parchment paper in an X-shape with ends that hang over the dish a little bit for easy lifting.

- In a large bowl, combine the cream cheese, mozzarella, crabmeat, scallions, agave, garlic powder, cayenne, soy sauce, Worcestershire, and salt. Gently stir to combine, trying not to break the crabmeat up too much.

- Press evenly into the prepared baking dish and place a piece of plastic wrap on top. Freeze for 30 minutes to 1 hour until the mixture is set and able to hold its shape.

- Set a wire rack in a sheet pan and have near the stove. Pour 2 to 3 inches canola oil into a large Dutch oven or heavy-bottomed pot and heat over medium-high to 365°F on a deep-fry thermometer.

- Remove the chilled cream cheese mixture from the baking dish to a cutting board. Cut in half, then cut each half into 8 sticks crosswise (you will have 16 sticks total).

- **Set up a dredging station with three shallow bowls:** In the first bowl add the flour. Add the eggs to the second. Place the panko in the third. Season each bowl generously with salt.

- Dip each mozzarella stick into the flour, shaking off any excess. Dip into the egg, and dredge in the panko. Working in batches to avoid overcrowding, fry a couple of sticks at a time until golden brown, 1 to 2 minutes. Using tongs, remove to the wire rack and season with salt.

- Serve with Thai sweet chili sauce.

- You can also make these in advance for easy recipe prep for a crowd. Simply prepare up to the freezing step. Wrap tightly and freeze for up to 1 day. Dredge and fry until golden brown. Because they are frozen, they may take a little longer to warm through. Serve.

Crab Rangoon Mozzarella Sticks

If you're looking for a dish that's the life of the party, these pulled pork nachos should be on your invite list. I may or may not know which teams are playing, but I do know these nachos are much more memorable than whether your favorite team is winning. They're the hot quarterback everyone can't keep their eyes off of . . . or their hands.

Pulled Pork

1 tablespoon light brown sugar

1½ tablespoons chili powder

2 teaspoons ground cumin

2 teaspoons ground coriander

1½ teaspoons garlic powder

1 teaspoon onion powder

2 teaspoons kosher salt

1 teaspoon freshly ground black pepper

2½ pounds boneless pork shoulder

2 tablespoons extra-virgin olive oil

1½ cups chicken broth

Queso

1 cup half-and-half

1 pound white American cheese, chopped

1 (4-ounce) can green chiles

1 teaspoon kosher salt

2 garlic cloves, grated

Nachos

1 (10-ounce) bag tortilla chips

1 (15.5-ounce) can black beans, drained and rinsed

1 bunch scallions, minced

½ cup pickled jalapeños, chopped

2 cups thinly sliced iceberg lettuce

2 Roma tomatoes, diced

1 cup sour cream

2 medium avocados, mashed

For Serving

3 limes, cut into wedges

Hot sauce

Spicy Homemade Ranch (page 263)

PREP
25 minutes

COOK
4 hours

SERVES
8

Game-Day Pulled Pork Nachos

● **Make the pulled pork:** Preheat the oven to 300°F.

● In a small bowl, stir together the brown sugar, chili powder, cumin, coriander, garlic powder, onion powder, salt, and pepper. Sprinkle evenly all over the pork.

● In a large Dutch oven or heavy-bottomed ovenproof pot, heat the olive oil over medium-high heat. Sear the pork on all sides until golden brown, 7 to 9 minutes. Add the chicken broth and bring to a simmer over medium heat, scraping any browned bits up from the bottom of the pan.

● Cover the pot with the lid and transfer to the oven to cook for 3 hours. Remove the lid and cook until the pork is very tender and can be shredded with a fork, about 1 hour longer. Shred the meat with two forks and set aside.

● **Make the queso:** In a medium saucepan, bring the half-and-half to a simmer over medium-low heat. Add the cheese and stir frequently until melted and smooth, about 3 minutes. Add the chiles, salt, and garlic, and stir again to combine. Set aside and keep warm.

● **Assemble the nachos:** Preheat the oven to 350°F.

● Spread the tortilla chips on a large sheet pan in an even layer. Top with the shredded pulled pork and black beans. Warm in the oven for 8 to 10 minutes. Top with warm queso.

● Garnish with the scallions, jalapeños, iceberg lettuce, tomatoes, sour cream, and mashed avocado. Serve with limes, hot sauce, and spicy homemade ranch on the side.

Game-Day
Pulled Pork
Nachos,
page 70

DIP
IT LOW

Living in Miami, I turn to this recipe as a go-to snack or appetizer for any pool party or beach day. Let's reveal how this dip came to be: Hummus seduced guacamole and on their way home, picked up a little lime, making the greatest flavor triangle yet. With punches of fresh lime and cilantro, it's a vibrant flavor with the silkiest of textures.

1 (15.5-ounce) can chickpeas, drained and rinsed

2 medium avocados, diced

¼ cup tahini

2 tablespoons extra-virgin olive oil, plus more for garnish

1 garlic clove, thinly sliced

Juice of 3 limes

½ teaspoon ground cumin

2 tablespoons fresh cilantro leaves, plus more for garnish

¼ teaspoon cayenne pepper

1 teaspoon kosher salt, plus more to taste

Freshly ground black pepper

Flaky sea salt, for garnish

For Serving

Za'atar Pita Chips (page 81)

Crackers

Rainbow carrots, halved lengthwise

Radishes, quartered if large

Sugar snap peas, ends trimmed

PREP
15 minutes

COOK
5 minutes

MAKES
3 cups
(Serves 6)

● In a medium saucepan, combine the chickpeas with water to cover. Bring to a simmer over medium-high heat and simmer until the chickpeas soften slightly, about 5 minutes. Reserving ½ cup of the hot cooking liquid, drain the chickpeas.

● In a food processor, combine the warm chickpeas, avocados, tahini, olive oil, garlic, and lime juice. Blend until smooth, adding ¼ cup of the reserved hot cooking water. Continue pulsing until the mixture is very smooth, light, and almost fluffy (adding more water as necessary).

● Add the cumin, cilantro, cayenne, and salt and pulse again until combined. Season with black pepper to taste.

● Swirl into a shallow bowl and garnish with additional cilantro leaves, a drizzle of olive oil, and flaky sea salt. Serve with pita chips, crackers, rainbow carrots, radishes, and sugar snap peas.

Avocado Hummus

This is a dip you most surely would find in heaven: luscious clouds of whipped creamy ricotta gathering pools of sweet and spicy honey. The food processor is your partner in crime to get that incredible texture. Slather onto grilled bread for a dip that is the definition of divine.

Whipped Ricotta

1 (16-ounce) container whole-milk ricotta

2 tablespoons extra-virgin olive oil

Grated zest of ½ lemon

1 teaspoon lemon juice

1 small garlic clove, roughly chopped

½ teaspoon kosher salt

2 tablespoons hot honey

For Garnish

Flaky sea salt

Aleppo pepper or red chile flakes

2 tablespoons chopped fresh chives

1 tablespoon extra-virgin olive oil

1 tablespoon hot honey

Grilled Bread

1 (16-ounce) loaf ciabatta, cut into ½-inch-thick slices

2 tablespoons extra-virgin olive oil

PREP
10 minutes

COOK
10 minutes

SERVES
4

● **Make the whipped ricotta:** In a food processor, combine the ricotta, olive oil, lemon zest, lemon juice, garlic, salt, and honey. Pulse until light, smooth, and airy, about 30 seconds.

● Remove the mixture to a shallow bowl and garnish with flaky sea salt, Aleppo pepper, the chives, olive oil, and hot honey.

● **Make the grilled bread:** Preheat the grill or grill pan to medium-high heat. Brush both sides of the bread with the olive oil. Grill on both sides until lightly charred, 1 to 2 minutes per side. Serve warm.

Whipped Ricotta & Hot Honey

Wake up and smell the herbs, am I right? This Creamy Herby Dip tastes like the queen you expect her to be: scrumptious, fresh, and oh-so creamy. It's one of those dips that's great to share or make on a Sunday to eat over the whole week. I love making Za'atar Pita Chips to serve alongside; they add an extra boost of super savory flavor to each bite.

½ cup fresh dill

⅓ cup fresh mint leaves

½ cup fresh parsley leaves

⅓ cup (packed) fresh basil leaves

2 garlic cloves, thinly sliced

3 scallions, chopped

¼ teaspoon ground coriander

Juice of 1 lemon

½ cup goat cheese (2 ounces), at room temperature

½ cup mayonnaise

¼ cup sour cream

2 teaspoons agave

1 teaspoon kosher salt

Freshly ground black pepper

Za'atar Pita Chips (recipe follows), for serving

PREP
10 minutes

MAKES
2 cups
(Serves 6)

● In a food processor, add the dill, mint, parsley, basil, garlic, and scallions. Pulse until finely chopped, scraping down the sides as needed.

● Add the coriander, lemon juice, goat cheese, mayonnaise, sour cream, agave, salt, and black pepper to taste. Blend until very smooth and bright green. Remove to a bowl and serve with the za'atar pita chips.

Make It Nice

Substitute ¾ cup reduced-fat plain Greek yogurt for the mayonnaise and sour cream. Follow the recipe as written.

ZA'ATAR PITA CHIPS

Makes 24 chips

3 pocketless pitas, each cut into 8 wedges

2 tablespoons extra-virgin olive oil

2 teaspoons za'atar

¼ teaspoon smoked paprika

Flaky sea salt

PREP
5 minutes

COOK
12 minutes

MAKES
24 chips

● Preheat the oven to 400°F. Line two baking sheets with parchment paper.

● Divide the pita wedges between the two baking sheets. Drizzle the pita with the olive oil and sprinkle with the za'atar, smoked paprika, and flaky salt.

● Bake until golden brown and toasted, 8 to 12 minutes.

● Allow to cool completely; they will continue to crisp as they cool.

Creamy Herby Dip

Just when you think life couldn't get better, let's take a trip to Bikini Bottom, where I hear The Krusty Krab serves the ultimate warm Crabby Patty Dip that may leave you hot and bothered. This dip has a creamy base loaded with fresh crabmeat that packs a kick thanks to Cajun seasoning and hot sauce. Plus, it's topped with one of my favorite crunchy ingredients: butter crackers. Warning: Your eyes might roll to the back of your head from the first bite.

Topping

2 tablespoons unsalted butter, melted

⅔ cup crushed butter crackers (about 14 crackers)

Kosher salt

Crabby Patty Dip

2 (8-ounce) packages cream cheese, at room temperature

⅓ cup sour cream

⅓ cup mayonnaise

3 scallions, finely chopped

2 teaspoons Worcestershire sauce

Grated zest and juice of 1 lemon

2½ teaspoons Old Bay seasoning

1 teaspoon Cajun seasoning

1 tablespoon hot sauce (I like Frank's)

⅔ cup grated yellow cheddar cheese

Kosher salt

1 pound jumbo lump crabmeat, picked over for shells

For Serving

2 scallions (green parts only), chopped, for garnish

Celery sticks

Carrot sticks

Butter crackers (I like Ritz)

Baguette, sliced on the bias

PREP
10 minutes

COOK
25 minutes

MAKES
5¼ cups
(Serves
8 to 10)

- **Make the topping:** In a medium bowl, stir together the melted butter, crushed butter crackers, and a pinch of salt and set aside.

- **Make the Crabby Patty dip:** Preheat the oven to 400°F.

- In a large bowl, mix together the cream cheese, sour cream, mayonnaise, scallions, Worcestershire sauce, lemon zest, lemon juice, Old Bay, Cajun seasoning, and hot sauce until very smooth.

- Add the cheddar, season with salt, and gently fold to combine. Add the crabmeat and gently fold together one last time, trying not to break up the lumps of crab too much.

- Place in a 1½-quart baking dish. Sprinkle the cracker topping on top.

- Bake until warmed through and bubbling, 20 to 25 minutes.

- **To serve:** Allow to cool for 10 minutes, then garnish with scallions. Serve with celery sticks, carrot sticks, butter crackers, and sliced baguette.

Crabby Patty Dip

Is there anything sexier than a French onion dip? Maybe a French kiss, but one might argue this dip is even better. This recipe happens to be extra luxurious thanks to the mascarpone cheese, aka cream cheese's bougie friend. The jammy onions are cooked with white wine for an extra glimmer of gourmet flavor to make it truly sparkle. The finishing touch is gooey Gruyère toasts, which are the definition of an ideal dipper.

2 tablespoons unsalted butter

2 large yellow onions (about 1 pound), thinly sliced (3 cups)

½ teaspoon dried thyme

Pinch of cayenne pepper

2 teaspoons kosher salt, plus more to taste

Freshly ground black pepper

⅓ cup dry white wine

4 ounces cream cheese, at room temperature

½ cup mayonnaise

1 (8-ounce) container mascarpone, at room temperature

1 teaspoon honey

2 teaspoons Worcestershire sauce

1 tablespoon chopped fresh parsley leaves

For Serving

1 baguette, cut into ½-inch-thick slices

1 cup grated Gruyère cheese

2 tablespoons thinly sliced fresh chives, for garnish

Potato chips

Endive leaves

Celery sticks

PREP
10 minutes, plus 1 hour chilling

COOK
30 minutes

MAKES
2½ cups (Serves 6)

● In a large skillet, heat the butter over medium-low heat. Add the onions, thyme, cayenne, 1 teaspoon of the salt, and pepper to taste and cook, stirring frequently, until just softened and starting to turn golden brown, about 10 minutes.

● Increase the heat to medium and deglaze with the white wine. Bring to a simmer and allow to reduce until the wine has evaporated. Continue to cook the onions, stirring often, until deep golden brown and jammy, another 15 to 20 minutes. Remove from the heat and allow to cool completely.

● When ready to assemble, in a large bowl, combine the cream cheese, mayonnaise, mascarpone, honey, and Worcestershire sauce. Using a hand mixer, beat on medium speed until light and fluffy, 1 to 2 minutes.

● Gently fold in the cooled caramelized onions and parsley. Season with the remaining 1 teaspoon salt. Refrigerate the dip for 30 minutes to 1 hour to thicken and set.

● **To serve:** When ready to serve, preheat the broiler. Arrange the baguette slices on a baking sheet and top with piles of Gruyère. Toast under the broiler until golden brown, bubbling, and melted, 2 to 3 minutes.

● Spoon the dip into a serving dish and garnish with chives. Serve with the warm Gruyère toasts, potato chips, endive leaves, and celery sticks.

Better Than a French Kiss Onion Dip

I LOVE elote. On the inside, she's sweet from each kernel of corn, but on the outside she's zesty, smoky, and spicy, giving you the best of both worlds. This dip gives elote a new flair with a creamy cheesy base that's so insanely addictive, you'll want to lick your plate. Don't skip grilling the corn—it takes this dip to a whole new level.

Grilled Corn

2 tablespoons extra-virgin olive oil

½ teaspoon ancho chile powder

½ teaspoon ground cumin

Pinch of cayenne pepper

3 to 4 ears corn, shucked

Kosher salt and freshly ground black pepper

Street Corn Dip

4 ounces cream cheese, at room temperature

1 (4-ounce) can green chiles

½ cup mayonnaise

½ cup sour cream

1½ cups grated pepper Jack cheese (6 ounces)

3 scallions, chopped

Grated zest of ½ lime

Juice of 1 lime

1 garlic clove, grated

Kosher salt and freshly ground black pepper

¼ cup crumbled Cotija cheese (1 ounce)

For Serving

¼ cup chopped fresh cilantro leaves, for garnish

Chile lime seasoning (I like Tajín)

Lime wedges

Tortilla chips

PREP
15 minutes

COOK
10 minutes

MAKES
3½ cups (Serves 6)

- **Make the grilled corn:** Preheat the grill or a grill pan to medium-high heat.

- In a small bowl, combine the olive oil, ancho powder, cumin, and cayenne and mix to combine. Brush onto the ears of corn and season with salt and pepper.

- Grill the corn on all sides until nicely charred, 5 to 8 minutes total. Set aside to cool slightly. Once cooled, cut the kernels off the cob (you should have about 2½ cups of kernels) and set aside.

- **Make the street corn dip:** Preheat the oven to 350°F.

- In a large bowl, combine the cream cheese, green chiles, mayonnaise, sour cream, ¾ cup of the pepper Jack, scallions, lime zest, lime juice, garlic, and three-quarters of the corn. Season with 1 teaspoon kosher salt and pepper to taste. Stir until well combined.

- Pour into a 1½-quart baking dish. Top with the remaining corn kernels, the Cotija, and remaining ¾ cup pepper Jack. Bake until warmed through and bubbling, 15 to 20 minutes.

- Turn the broiler to high and allow the top to broil until lightly golden, another 3 to 4 minutes.

- **To serve:** Allow to cool for 10 minutes before serving. Garnish with cilantro and chile lime seasoning. Serve with lime wedges and tortilla chips.

Grilled Mexican Street Corn Dip

Oh, pimento cheese, your sweet Southernness has stolen my heart. Don't be fooled by this classic recipe: It seems simple and unassuming, but it's sure to be your new favorite dip or condiment to add to sandwiches, crackers, and even elbows for a mac and cheese that will leave you speechless. My secret compared to the classic recipe is adding a hint of barbecue sauce for a little smoky sweet flavor.

- In a large bowl, combine the cream cheese, mayonnaise, barbecue sauce, Worcestershire sauce, mustard, garlic powder, onion powder, cayenne, salt, and black pepper. Mix until well combined.

- Add the cheddar and pimentos and fold gently until combined. Season again to taste.

- **To serve:** Garnish with chives and serve alongside crackers, baguette, and celery sticks.

1 (8-ounce) package cream cheese, at room temperature

¾ cup mayonnaise

2 teaspoons barbecue sauce

1 teaspoon Worcestershire sauce

1 teaspoon yellow mustard

½ teaspoon garlic powder

½ teaspoon onion powder

Pinch of cayenne pepper

1 teaspoon kosher salt

¼ teaspoon freshly ground black pepper

4¾ cups grated extra-sharp yellow cheddar cheese (1 pound 3 ounces)

¾ cup jarred pimentos, finely chopped

PREP
15 minutes

MAKES
6 cups
(Serves 12)

For Serving

1 tablespoon chopped fresh chives, for garnish

Butter crackers

Baguette slices

Celery sticks

Southern-Style Pimento Cheese Dip

This guacamole is so addicting. Before you know it, you will have scooped all the way to the bottom of the bowl. The base of the guacamole is classic with cilantro, jalapeño, and lime juice. I like to be a little playful and add some delicious caramelized grilled peaches, tangy pomegranate seeds, and even some feta to make your taste buds dance.

1½ teaspoons unsalted butter

1 peach, diced

1½ teaspoons light brown sugar

4 avocados, cut into large pieces

½ small red onion, finely diced

¼ cup fresh cilantro leaves, chopped

1 jalapeño, seeded and finely diced

2 garlic cloves, minced

Juice of 1 lime

½ teaspoon kosher salt

¾ cup pomegranate seeds

For Serving

Chopped fresh cilantro, for garnish

¼ cup crumbled feta (optional), for garnish

Tortilla chips

Rainbow carrots, halved lengthwise

Endive leaves

PREP
15 minutes

COOK
6 minutes

MAKES
4 cups
(Serves 6)

● In a medium skillet, heat the butter over medium heat until melted. Add the peaches and brown sugar and cook until the peaches have softened and are lightly caramelized, 4 to 6 minutes. Remove the peaches to a small bowl and allow to cool in the fridge while you make the guacamole.

● In a large bowl, roughly mash the avocados with a fork. Add the onion, cilantro, jalapeño, garlic, lime juice, and salt and mash to combine.

● Add three-quarters of the pomegranate seeds as well as three-quarters of the cooled peaches and gently stir to combine.

● **To serve:** Transfer to a serving bowl and top with the remaining pomegranate seeds, peaches, and more cilantro. Top with crumbled feta if you're feeling naughty! Serve with tortilla chips, rainbow carrots, and endive leaves.

Make It Nice

Reduce the avocados to 3. Add ⅔ cup 2% Greek yogurt to the avocado mixture and stir well until whipped and incorporated. Continue the recipe as written.

Caramelized Peach & Pomegranate Guacamole

This dipping oil is a slippery slope to insane flavor. With a kick of spice, a punch of herby deliciousness, and a zing of garlic, it's the ideal way to start off a date night at home when you're ready to impress your latest crush. Serve with warm, fluffy bread to sop up every last drop.

1 teaspoon dried thyme

1 teaspoon dried oregano

½ teaspoon dried rosemary

1 tablespoon jarred chopped Calabrian chili peppers

½ cup good-quality extra-virgin olive oil

4 large garlic cloves, thinly sliced

2 tablespoons freshly grated Parmesan cheese

2 tablespoons finely chopped fresh parsley

Flaky sea salt and freshly ground black pepper

Ciabatta or baguette, cut into ½-inch-thick slices and warmed, for serving

PREP
10 minutes

COOK
3 minutes

MAKES
⅔ cup

● In a heatproof medium bowl, combine the thyme, oregano, rosemary, and Calabrian chili peppers. Set aside. Line a small plate with paper towels.

● In a small skillet, warm the olive oil and garlic over low heat until the garlic infuses the olive oil and is aromatic and golden brown, 2 to 3 minutes. Using a slotted spoon, remove the golden brown garlic chips to the paper towels to cool and crisp.

● Let the olive oil cool for 5 minutes, then pour over the spice mixture in the bowl to infuse the flavors. Allow the olive oil to cool to room temperature.

● Transfer to a serving bowl and top with the garlic chips, Parmesan, parsley, and flaky sea salt and black pepper to taste. Serve with warmed bread for dipping.

Restaurant-Style Dipping Oil with Calabrian Chilies

LEAF ME WANTING MORE

This is for the people who love the toppings of the salad more than the lettuce itself. I am her, she is me. Lettuce is great and all, but this baby focuses on all of the crunchies on top. She's dressed in my beautiful Green Goddess Dressing with alllll the herbs, for a kiss of freshness in each bite. This is a salad that stores well for a day or two, so make a batch and keep it for an easy lunch.

⅓ cup sliced almonds

½ small head green cabbage (about 1¼ pounds), cored

1 bunch of scallions

3 cups Brussels sprouts (15 ounces), ends trimmed

3 Persian (mini) cucumbers, finely diced

⅓ cup dried cranberries

1 green bell pepper, diced

1 avocado, diced

⅓ cup sesame sticks

Green Goddess Dressing (recipe follows)

Kosher salt and freshly ground black pepper

Pita or tortilla chips, for serving

PREP
15 minutes

COOK
4 minutes

SERVES
4

- In a small skillet, toast the sliced almonds over medium-low heat until lightly golden, 3 to 4 minutes. Place in a bowl to cool immediately. Set aside.

- Finely chop the cabbage and scallions and place in a large bowl. Thinly slice the Brussels sprouts using a knife or a mandoline. If you don't want to use a knife, you can easily do the chopping and shredding in the food processor. Just be sure to pulse the vegetables in batches and place in a large bowl.

- Add the cucumbers, cranberries, bell pepper, avocado, sesame sticks, and toasted almonds and toss to combine. Drizzle the Green Goddess Dressing around the rim of the bowl and toss to evenly coat. Season with salt and pepper to taste.

- Serve the salad with pita or tortilla chips for scooping.

GREEN GODDESS DRESSING

Makes 1 cup

2 garlic cloves, chopped
1 small shallot, chopped
Juice of 1 lemon
¼ cup roughly chopped fresh chives
¼ cup nondairy yogurt
1 cup baby spinach
2 tablespoons extra-virgin olive oil
½ cup (packed) fresh basil leaves
1 tablespoon agave
½ teaspoon Worcestershire sauce (optional)
½ teaspoon kosher salt
Freshly ground black pepper

- In a high-powered blender, combine the garlic, shallot, lemon juice, chives, yogurt, spinach, olive oil, basil, agave, Worcestershire sauce (if using), and salt. Blend until combined and smooth, about 10 seconds. Season with pepper to taste. Store in an airtight container for up to 5 days in the fridge.

All the Crunchies Salad

When I'm craving a Big Mac, I think of late Saturday nights when my inhibitions are low and my desires take over, aka I'm going through that drive-thru. Luckily, I found a way to make it at home without the guilt and all the same delicious flavors. This twist takes the classic Big Mac burger to the world of chopped salads—even the salad haters will be converted. Be warned, this salad will definitely be added to your weekly meal rotation.

Sesame Croutons

2 cups ¾-inch cubes Italian bread

3 tablespoons unsalted butter, melted

Kosher salt

1 tablespoon sesame seeds

Seasoned Beef

1 tablespoon extra-virgin olive oil

1 pound lean ground beef

1 teaspoon paprika

1 teaspoon garlic powder

1 teaspoon onion powder

2 garlic cloves, minced

1 teaspoon kosher salt

Freshly ground black pepper

2 tablespoons ketchup

Salad

2 heads romaine (12 ounces total), cored and chopped (about 5 cups)

1 tomato, seeded and diced

½ red onion, diced

½ cup chopped dill pickles

1 cup grated sharp yellow cheddar cheese

Golden Arches Sauce (page 259)

PREP
15 minutes

COOK
35 minutes

SERVES
4

● **Make the sesame croutons:** Preheat the oven to 350°F. Line a baking sheet with parchment paper.

● In a large bowl, combine the bread cubes, melted butter, and salt to taste and toss to coat. Evenly spread onto the prepared baking sheet. Sprinkle with the sesame seeds.

● Bake until golden brown and toasted, 10 to 15 minutes, tossing halfway through. Set aside to cool.

● **Make the seasoned beef:** In a large skillet, heat the olive oil over medium-high heat. Add the beef and allow to cook without moving until browned on one side, about 3 minutes.

● Sprinkle the beef with the paprika, garlic powder, onion powder, minced garlic, salt, and pepper to taste. Add the ketchup and begin breaking up the beef with a wooden spoon into crumbles. Continue cooking, stirring occasionally, until browned and fully cooked through, about 4 minutes. Set aside and keep warm.

● **Make the salad:** Add the chopped romaine to a large serving bowl or four individual bowls. Top with the warm seasoned beef, tomato, onion, dill pickles, cheddar, and sesame croutons. Drizzle with the Golden Arches Sauce and serve.

The Mac Salad

This salad is giving big spoon energy. We've got fresh crunchy veggies, a zesty lemon oregano vinaigrette, and smokin' hot orzo pasta that soaks up all of that delicious flavor. And just like a big spoon, you'll never get enough of it.

Kosher salt

1 cup orzo pasta (about 6 ounces)

Greek Dressing

Juice of 1 lemon

2 tablespoons white wine vinegar

⅓ cup extra-virgin olive oil

1 teaspoon agave

2 garlic cloves, grated

½ teaspoon dried oregano

Pinch of red chile flakes

½ teaspoon kosher salt, plus more to taste

Freshly ground black pepper

Salad

1 cup cherry tomatoes, halved

4 ounces feta cheese, crumbled (about 1 cup)

1 preserved lemon, chopped

½ English cucumber, cut into ¼-inch-thick half-moons

½ small red onion, thinly sliced

¼ cup pitted kalamata olives, chopped

¼ cup fresh dill

¼ cup fresh basil leaves, torn

¼ cup fresh mint leaves, chopped

2 cups baby arugula

Kosher salt and freshly ground black pepper

PREP
15 minutes, plus chilling time

COOK
15 minutes

SERVES
6

● Bring a large pot of salted water to a boil over high heat. Add the orzo and cook according to the package directions for al dente.

● **Meanwhile, make the Greek dressing:** In a large bowl, whisk together the lemon juice, vinegar, olive oil, agave, garlic, oregano, chile flakes, salt, and pepper to taste.

● Drain the orzo, and while it's still warm, add it to the dressing and toss to coat. This allows the pasta to sop up all the flavors of the dressing even more. Set aside to cool to room temperature for 10 minutes.

● **Assemble the salad:** Add the cherry tomatoes, feta, preserved lemon, cucumber, red onion, olives, dill, basil, and mint. Toss until everything is evenly combined. Refrigerate if desired for 30 minutes before serving to allow the flavors to meld.

● When ready to serve, add the arugula and fold into the pasta to combine. Season with salt and pepper to taste and serve.

Lemon Greek Orzo Salad

This is one of those salads I crave every single week. It's turning your favorite takeout into an easy version made right at home. I love adding crispy tofu on top for a bite of protein that takes on all the peanutty flavors of the dressing. It's also delicious with chicken, steak, and shrimp.

Crispy Tofu

1 (12- to 15-ounce) block extra-firm tofu

1 tablespoon tamari

2 tablespoons cornstarch

2 tablespoons avocado oil

Kosher salt

Peanut Noodle Salad

6 ounces pad Thai rice noodles

Ginger Peanut Sauce (page 267)

3½ cups shaved red cabbage (10½ ounces)

1 cup julienned carrots (4 to 5 medium)

1 cup sugar snap peas, ends trimmed and cut in half on the bias

½ bunch of scallions, thinly sliced

¼ cup fresh cilantro leaves

¼ cup fresh mint leaves, chopped

½ cup salted roasted cashews, chopped

Lime wedges, for serving

PREP
30 minutes

COOK
10 minutes

SERVES
4 to 6

● **Make the crispy tofu:** Set the tofu on a plate lined with paper towels. Place another piece of paper towel on top of the tofu as well as another plate and press the plate down with a heavy pot or canned goods. Allow the tofu to be pressed for 10 minutes to release excess liquid.

● Once the tofu is pressed, cut it into 1-inch cubes and place in a large bowl. Toss with the tamari and cornstarch to coat.

● Line a new plate with paper towels and have near the stove. In a large nonstick skillet, heat the avocado oil over medium-high heat. Once the oil is hot, add the tofu and cook on all sides until golden brown, 6 to 9 minutes total. Remove the tofu to the paper towels and season with salt.

● **Make the peanut noodle salad:** Bring a medium saucepan of water to a boil. Add the noodles and cook according to the package directions for al dente. Drain and rinse the noodles under cold water until room temperature, then add to the large bowl with the ginger peanut sauce.

● Add the red cabbage, carrots, snap peas, scallions, cilantro, mint, and cashews and toss to combine.

● Divide among shallow bowls and top with crispy tofu. Serve with lime wedges.

● Store any leftovers in an airtight container in the fridge for up to 3 days.

Thai Peanut Noodle Salad with Crispy Tofu

I have a dirty secret: This pizza salad is best enjoyed all alone as a party of one. It's so addictive, you may just want to eat every last bite. The pizza dough on the bottom cradles the sultry chopped salad on top and also absorbs that delicious zesty dressing, ultimately making it the best tearable breadstick out there. A bite of all the flavors together truly has me saying "that's amore."

Zesty Italian Vinaigrette

⅓ cup red wine vinegar

1 garlic clove, grated

1 small shallot, minced

½ teaspoon Italian seasoning

1 teaspoon agave

Pinch of red chile flakes

⅓ cup extra-virgin olive oil

Kosher salt and freshly ground black pepper

Seasoned Pizza Crust

3 tablespoons extra-virgin olive oil

1 pound refrigerated pizza dough, at room temperature

¼ cup freshly grated Parmesan cheese

1½ teaspoons Italian seasoning

Kosher salt and freshly ground black pepper

Chopped Italian Salad

1 head romaine lettuce (6 ounces), chopped

8 ounces fresh mozzarella pearls

1 cup cherry tomatoes, halved

½ cup pepperoncini peppers, chopped

4 ounces salami, chopped into ½-inch pieces

2 ounces pepperoni, chopped

2 tablespoons freshly grated Parmesan cheese

¼ cup fresh basil leaves, torn

PREP
25 minutes

COOK
15 minutes

SERVES
6

RECIPE
CONTINUES

Chopped Italian Salad Pizza

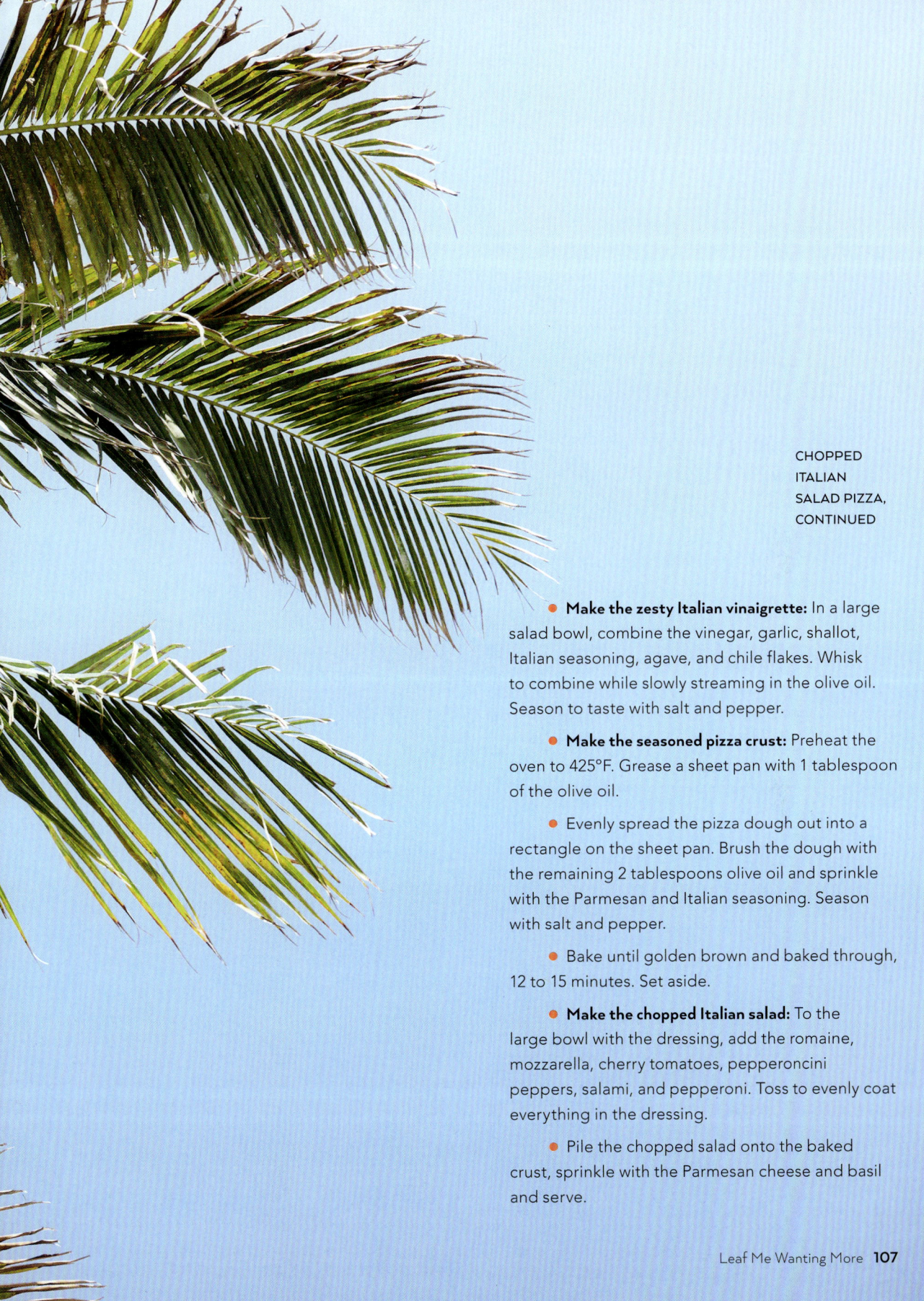

CHOPPED
ITALIAN
SALAD PIZZA,
CONTINUED

● **Make the zesty Italian vinaigrette:** In a large salad bowl, combine the vinegar, garlic, shallot, Italian seasoning, agave, and chile flakes. Whisk to combine while slowly streaming in the olive oil. Season to taste with salt and pepper.

● **Make the seasoned pizza crust:** Preheat the oven to 425°F. Grease a sheet pan with 1 tablespoon of the olive oil.

● Evenly spread the pizza dough out into a rectangle on the sheet pan. Brush the dough with the remaining 2 tablespoons olive oil and sprinkle with the Parmesan and Italian seasoning. Season with salt and pepper.

● Bake until golden brown and baked through, 12 to 15 minutes. Set aside.

● **Make the chopped Italian salad:** To the large bowl with the dressing, add the romaine, mozzarella, cherry tomatoes, pepperoncini peppers, salami, and pepperoni. Toss to evenly coat everything in the dressing.

● Pile the chopped salad onto the baked crust, sprinkle with the Parmesan cheese and basil and serve.

Here's to our mermaid moment. This salad is basically the equivalent of a seafood tower in lettuce form. Inspired by the crazed Lobster Cobb at Duryea's in Montauk, Long Island, this is my version complete with my Green Goddess Dressing and Old Bay bread crumbs. One bite will have you saying "chef's kiss" . . . or maybe kiss the chef?

Old Bay Panko Bread Crumbs

2 tablespoons unsalted butter

½ cup panko bread crumbs

1 teaspoon Old Bay seasoning

Kosher salt

Lobster Salad

2 large eggs

4 heads Little Gem lettuce (1 pound total), leaves separated

2 tablespoons chopped fresh tarragon leaves

5 slices bacon, cooked and chopped

2 celery stalks, thinly sliced

¼ cup grated white cheddar cheese

1 cup cherry tomatoes, halved

1 small avocado, diced

1 pound cooked lobster meat, chopped

½ recipe Green Goddess Dressing (page 97)

Lemon wedges, for serving

PREP
30 minutes

COOK
15 minutes

SERVES
4 to 6

● **Make the Old Bay bread crumbs:** Line a plate with paper towels. In a medium skillet, melt the butter over medium-low heat. Add the panko and Old Bay and stir to combine. Toast until golden brown, stirring frequently, 3 to 4 minutes. Remove to the paper towels and season with a pinch of salt. Allow to cool to room temperature.

● **Make the lobster salad:** Fill a large saucepan with water and bring to a boil over high heat. Add the eggs and reduce the heat to medium. Boil for 10 minutes and then drain. When they are cool enough to handle, peel and quarter the eggs.

● In a large bowl, combine the Little Gem lettuce and tarragon. Top with the cooked bacon, celery, cheddar, tomatoes, avocado, and egg quarters. In the center of the salad, mound the lobster meat in a large pile. Drizzle with the Green Goddess Dressing and Old Bay bread crumbs. Serve with lemon wedges.

Lobster Cobb Salad

Grab the ripest watermelon you can find; you'll want to make sure it's extra juicy so that it's perfect for this salad. Pair that natural red sweetness with some salty feta, fresh mint, and basil, for a flavor explosion. My naughty little secret here is marinating the red onions in rice vinegar and a hint of sesame oil. Its subtle richness balances the bite of the raw onions (although a little nibble never hurt anyone).

Honey Lime Dressing

Juice of 2 limes

1 tablespoon honey

⅓ cup extra-virgin olive oil

Kosher salt and freshly ground
   black pepper

Salad

½ small red onion, thinly sliced

¼ cup rice vinegar

1 teaspoon toasted sesame oil

1 ripe mini watermelon
   (4 to 5 pounds), cubed
   (8 to 9 cups)

2 medium heirloom tomatoes,
   cut into ½-inch-thick wedges

½ cup packed fresh basil
   leaves, torn

¼ cup packed fresh mint
   leaves, torn

1 (4-ounce) block feta cheese,
   cut into ½-inch cubes

1 avocado, diced

Grated zest of 1 lime

½ teaspoon ground sumac

Flaky sea salt

PREP
15 minutes

SERVES
6

● **Make the honey lime dressing:** In a medium bowl, whisk together the lime juice and honey, then whisk in the olive oil. Season with salt and pepper to taste.

● **Assemble the salad:** In a small bowl, stir together the red onion, vinegar, and sesame oil and set aside to marinate for 10 minutes.

● In a large bowl, combine the watermelon, tomatoes, basil, mint, feta, avocado, and marinated red onions. Drizzle with the dressing and gently toss to coat.

● Transfer to a serving bowl and sprinkle with the lime zest, sumac, and flaky sea salt.

Watermelon & Feta Salad

So can we all agree that Caesar salad is only made better when it's paired with a nood? Fusilli is my choice, thanks to its curly edges that get wonderfully coated in all that creamy dressing. To top it off, toasted croissants make the most INSANE croutons—flaky, crunchy layers of buttery deliciousness. Each bite of this salad makes for lip-smacking goodness.

2 croissants, cut into 1-inch cubes

1 tablespoon unsalted butter, melted

Kosher salt and freshly ground black pepper

1 cup fusilli pasta

2 heads romaine lettuce (12 ounces total), chopped (about 5 cups)

¼ cup freshly grated Parmesan cheese, plus more (optional) for garnish

2 tablespoons capers, drained and chopped

Caesar Dressing (recipe follows)

PREP
15 minutes

COOK
12 minutes

SERVES
4

● Preheat the oven to 375°F. Line a baking sheet with parchment paper.

● Arrange the croissant cubes on the baking sheet and drizzle with the melted butter. Season with salt and pepper and toss to evenly coat. Bake until deep golden brown and nicely toasted, 10 to 12 minutes, stirring halfway through. Set aside to cool.

● Meanwhile, bring a large pot of salted water to a boil over high heat. Add the fusilli and cook according to the package directions for al dente. Drain and rinse under cold water until room temperature.

● In a large bowl, combine the cooked pasta, romaine, Parmesan, and capers. Drizzle the dressing around the rim of the bowl, then toss to evenly combine (this ensures the salad is evenly dressed).

● Add the croutons and toss again lightly to combine. Serve with additional Parmesan cheese grated on top if desired.

CAESAR DRESSING
Makes ⅔ cup

1 small garlic clove, grated
1 anchovy fillet
Juice of ½ lemon
½ teaspoon Worcestershire sauce
¼ cup mayonnaise
1 tablespoon extra-virgin olive oil
¼ cup freshly grated Parmesan cheese
¼ teaspoon kosher salt
Freshly ground black pepper

● In a small food processor, combine the garlic, anchovy, lemon juice, Worcestershire sauce, mayonnaise, olive oil, Parmesan, salt, and pepper to taste. Blend until very smooth.

Caesar Pasta Salad with Croissant Croutons

This salad is one that's inspired by the classic Italian appetizer of melon and prosciutto. We're just giving it that hot girl summer spin. Pull out that melon baller—it's so easy to use and gives this salad a sassy presentation. A bed of peppery arugula complements that natural fruity sweetness of the honeydew, with a punch of meaty saltiness from the crispy prosciutto.

1 (4-ounce) package thinly sliced prosciutto

2 cups baby arugula

1 honeydew melon (4 pounds), seeded and scooped into balls using a melon baller (about 9 cups)

1 cup mozzarella ciliegine (about 8 ounces)

1 cup basil leaves, torn

2 tablespoons hot honey

1 tablespoon white wine vinegar

2 tablespoons extra-virgin olive oil

½ teaspoon kosher salt, plus more to taste

Freshly ground black pepper

Flaky sea salt

PREP
20 minutes

COOK
12 minutes

SERVES
6

- Preheat the oven to 400°F. Line a baking sheet with parchment paper.

- Lay out the strips of prosciutto on the baking sheet and bake until golden brown and the fat has rendered, 9 to 12 minutes. Allow to cool for 5 minutes; the prosciutto will continue to crisp.

- In a large bowl, combine the baby arugula, honeydew melon, mozzarella ciliegine, and basil leaves. Set aside.

- In a small bowl, whisk together the hot honey, vinegar, and olive oil. Season with the salt and pepper to taste. Drizzle over the melon and greens and toss to evenly coat and combine everything.

- Place the salad on a large serving platter. Break the crispy prosciutto into pieces and place on top of the salad. Sprinkle with flaky sea salt and a fresh grinding of black pepper and serve.

Honeydew & Mozzarella Salad with Crispy Prosciutto

GET YOUR HANDS DIRTY

This sammy is truly a workout—for your mouth, that is. Loaded with ribbons of luscious mortadella, prosciutto, and salami and slathered with a cherry pepper spread that you should have on hand every day of the week. A shower of fresh Italian chopped salad keeps things crunchy, just the way I like it.

Cherry Pepper & Pepperoncini Spread

½ cup pickled cherry peppers

½ cup pepperoncini

1 garlic clove, sliced

1 teaspoon agave

Kosher salt and freshly ground black pepper

Hoagie Sandwich

1 (12-inch) giant hoagie roll or 2 (6- to 8-inch) medium hoagie rolls, split horizontally

2 tablespoons mayonnaise

¼ pound thinly sliced provolone

½ pound thinly sliced genoa salami

½ pound thinly sliced mortadella

½ pound thinly sliced prosciutto

2 cups shredded iceberg lettuce

½ recipe Red Wine Vinaigrette (recipe follows)

PREP
15 minutes

COOK
2 minutes

MAKES
4 sandwiches

● **Make the cherry pepper & pepperoncini spread:** In a food processor, combine the cherry peppers, pepperoncini, garlic, and agave. Pulse until finely chopped and a jam-like consistency forms. Season to taste with salt and pepper. Set aside. You can store in an airtight container in the fridge for up to 1 week.

● **Make the hoagie sandwich:** Position a rack in the top third of the oven and preheat the broiler.

● On a baking sheet, split the hoagie roll(s) open and spread the mayonnaise evenly inside.

● Shingle the provolone over the side of the rolls that will be the top side of the sandwich and place under the broiler for 1 to 2 minutes to toast the bread and melt the cheese (be careful, as all broilers vary in strength!). Remove from the oven.

● Spread the bottom side of the hoagie roll (the side without cheese) with the cherry pepper and pepperoncini spread. Layer the bottom side of the hoagie roll with the salami, mortadella, and prosciutto.

● In a medium bowl, toss the iceberg lettuce with the red wine vinaigrette to evenly coat. Place the iceberg on top of the prosciutto and sandwich both sides of the roll together. Cut in quarters, if using a longer roll, or halves, if using 2 rolls, and serve immediately.

RED WINE VINAIGRETTE

Makes scant ½ cup

1 teaspoon Dijon mustard

2 tablespoons red wine vinegar

1 teaspoon agave

1 teaspoon Italian seasoning

⅓ cup extra-virgin olive oil

Kosher salt and freshly ground black pepper

● In a small bowl, whisk together the mustard, vinegar, agave, and Italian seasoning until well combined. While constantly whisking, slowly stream in the olive oil until an emulsified dressing forms. Season to taste with salt and pepper.

Loaded Italian Sandwich

This is one of those perfect spring or summer brunch, lunch, or truly anytime sandwiches. It's the definition of sexy in each bite. Fresh berries are dressed in a blanket of ooey, gooey Fontina and Gouda with a kiss of truffle and honey.

Mixed Berry Jam

1 (6-ounce) container raspberries

1 (6-ounce) container blackberries

Juice of 1 lemon

1 tablespoon honey

2 teaspoons cornstarch

1 teaspoon fresh thyme leaves

Grilled Cheese

4 tablespoons (2 ounces) unsalted butter, at room temperature

8 slices sourdough bread

8 slices Gouda cheese

8 slices Fontina cheese

4 teaspoons white truffle oil

2 tablespoons honey, plus more for garnish

PREP
10 minutes

COOK
10 minutes

MAKES
4 sandwiches

● **Make the mixed berry jam:** In a medium saucepan, combine the raspberries, blackberries, lemon juice, and honey. Bring to a simmer over medium-low heat. Allow the berries to break down, about 4 minutes, then use the back of a spoon to mash into a jam-like consistency (not too fine, I like some texture).

● In a small bowl, stir together 1 tablespoon water and the cornstarch. Add the cornstarch slurry and thyme leaves to the jam and stir to combine. Bring to a simmer over medium-low heat and allow to thicken slightly, another minute or so. Set aside and allow to cool (it will continue to thicken).

● **Make the grilled cheese:** Heat a large cast-iron or nonstick skillet over medium-low heat. Butter one side of each piece of bread.

● Place 2 pieces of the bread into the skillet, buttered-side down. Top each piece of bread with 1 slice Gouda and 1 slice Fontina. Spoon over a heaping tablespoon of the jam on each piece of bread. Drizzle each sandwich with 1 teaspoon truffle oil and 1½ teaspoons honey, and top each with another slice of Fontina and Gouda. Add a second piece of bread on top, buttered-side up.

● Once the bottom slice of bread is golden brown, about 3 minutes, flip and allow the other side to brown and the cheese to melt, another 2 to 3 minutes. Remove from the pan and let the sandwiches rest for 5 minutes. Repeat with the remaining ingredients to make 2 more sandwiches (a total of 4).

● Slice and serve with another drizzle of honey and more mixed berry jam on the side.

Truffle Honey Berry Grilled Cheese

You know when you dunk a crusty, warm piece of baguette into the gooiest, jammiest French onion soup? That bite always transports me right to my favorite bistro in Paris. This garlic bread is the sandwich version of that moment, meant to take you right to the market streets of the beautiful city, walking along the Seine, and saying "c'est la vie."

Roasted Garlic Butter

2 heads garlic

1 tablespoon extra-virgin olive oil

4 tablespoons (2 ounces) unsalted butter, at room temperature

Caramelized Onions

2 tablespoons unsalted butter

1 tablespoon extra-virgin olive oil

2 large yellow onions (about 1¼ pounds total), thinly sliced

2 teaspoons fresh thyme

1 teaspoon kosher salt

Béchamel

2 tablespoons unsalted butter

2 tablespoons all-purpose flour

1 cup whole milk

½ teaspoon kosher salt, plus more to taste

Freshly ground black pepper

½ cup freshly grated Gruyère cheese

Garlic Bread

1 large Italian loaf or demi baguette, split in half lengthwise

½ cup grated Gruyère cheese

1 teaspoon fresh thyme, for garnish

PREP
15 minutes

COOK
1 hour
20 minutes

SERVES
4

RECIPE
CONTINUES

Caramelized Onion Garlic Bread

● **Make the roasted garlic butter:** Preheat the oven to 400°F.

● Cut the top third off of each head of garlic to expose the tops of the cloves. Drizzle the olive oil over the 2 heads. Place the garlic heads in a sheet of foil and wrap to fully enclose.

● Roast until the garlic cloves are tender, golden brown, and caramelized, 50 minutes to 1 hour. Remove from the oven, but leave the oven on for the garlic bread.

● Set the garlic aside and allow to cool. Once cooled, mash the garlic cloves and stir them into the softened butter and set aside.

● **Meanwhile, make the caramelized onions:** In a large skillet, heat the butter and olive oil over medium heat. Add the onions and cook until softened with little to no color, 5 to 7 minutes.

● Add the thyme and salt and continue stirring. Cook the onions, constantly stirring, until they are deep golden brown and caramelized, 35 to 40 minutes. If the onions ever feel like they may burn, just add a splash of water and continue cooking. Remove the onions from the pan and set aside to cool (you'll have about 1½ cups).

● **Make the béchamel:** In a medium saucepan, melt the butter over medium-low heat. Once melted, stir in the flour and cook until a paste forms, about 1 minute. While whisking constantly, slowly stream the milk into the flour paste. Whisk well so all the lumps are removed. Season with the salt and pepper to taste.

● Bring the mixture to a simmer over medium heat and whisk constantly until thickened, 3 to 5 minutes. The key to knowing a béchamel is finished is by dipping a spoon into the sauce and running your finger through the sauce on the back of the spoon. If the sauce doesn't run together on the spoon, it's finished.

● Remove the sauce from the heat and let it cool for 10 minutes. Stir in the caramelized onions and Gruyère and set aside.

● **Make the garlic bread:** Place a rack in the top third of the oven. (It should already be at 400°F, but if not, preheat.)

● Evenly spread both sides of the bread with the garlic butter. Place on a baking sheet and toast in the oven until golden brown, 5 to 7 minutes.

● Remove from the oven and preheat the broiler. Evenly spoon the caramelized onion béchamel over both sides of the bread. Sprinkle with the Gruyère.

● Place under the broiler for 1 to 2 minutes until the cheese is bubbling and golden brown. Remove from the oven and allow to cool for 5 minutes. Garnish with thyme, then slice into 4 pieces and serve.

I'm not sure if there's anything better than a medium-rare steak sandwich drooling with drippings on a cloud of garlicky aioli and caramelized onions. And we're using the king of all steaks, filet mignon. Get ready to cook to impress. This will score a 10/10 on a first date, is perfect to feed a crowd, or is also ideal for a night that's all about me, myself, and I.

Caramelized Onions

1 tablespoon extra-virgin olive oil

2 tablespoons unsalted butter

2 large Vidalia onions, thinly sliced

½ teaspoon kosher salt

1 tablespoon Worcestershire sauce

1 teaspoon fresh thyme

Filet Mignon

2 filet mignon steaks (8 ounces each)

Kosher salt and freshly ground black pepper

2 tablespoons extra-virgin olive oil

3 garlic cloves, peeled and left whole

1 sprig rosemary

1 tablespoon unsalted butter

Assembly

1 loaf crusty bread, cut into ¾-inch-thick slices and toasted

Garlic Dijonnaise (recipe follows)

2 cups baby arugula

1 cup store-bought fried onions

PREP
20 minutes

COOK
1 hour

MAKES
4 sandwiches

RECIPE
CONTINUES

The Ultimate Steak Sandwich

● **Make the caramelized onions:** In a large skillet, heat the olive oil and butter over medium-low heat. Add the onions and salt and stir frequently until deep golden brown and caramelized, about 30 minutes. During the last 5 minutes, add the Worcestershire sauce and thyme and stir to combine. Set aside to cool.

● **Cook the filet mignon:** Let the steaks sit out at room temperature for 20 minutes for even cooking.

● Pat the steaks dry on both sides with paper towels and season with salt and pepper. In a large cast-iron skillet, heat the olive oil over high heat. Sear the steaks until deep golden brown and medium-rare or 125°F on a meat thermometer, about 3 minutes per side (see Note). When you flip the steaks, add the garlic, rosemary, and butter. Once the butter melts, spoon it over the steaks a couple of times.

● Remove the steaks from the skillet and allow them to rest for 10 minutes. Thinly slice the steak against the grain into slices a little less than ½ inch thick.

● **Assemble the sandwiches:** On the toasted bread, schmear garlic Dijonnaise on one side of both slices. Top with slices of steak, caramelized onions, arugula, and crispy fried onions. Add the top slice of bread, slice in half, and serve.

● You can store all of the components of this sandwich for leftovers easily. Simply place the caramelized onions, Dijonnaise, and steak in separate airtight containers. Store in the fridge for up to 3 days. Reheat the steak carefully in the microwave for 1 to 2 minutes or in a 300°F oven until just warmed through. Layer the sandwich.

Note

If your steaks are on the thicker side, you will want to finish them in the oven after searing to get to the correct medium-rare temperature. Preheat the oven to 425°F. After searing the steaks on both sides, transfer the skillet to the oven to cook until the steaks register 125°F on a meat thermometer, 3 to 6 minutes.

GARLIC DIJONNAISE

Makes ⅔ cup

½ cup mayonnaise
4 garlic cloves, grated
1 tablespoon fresh lemon juice
1 tablespoon Dijon mustard
Kosher salt

● In a medium bowl, stir together the mayonnaise, garlic, lemon juice, mustard, and salt. Mix until combined and smooth.

What happens when a Big Mac and tacos walk into a bar? They leave together in a smashing romance, creating a merriment of ingredients and heart-wrenching flavors. The beef is smashed against the tortilla on the griddle to make some nice crispy edges. As a result, the tortilla gets crispy and truly becomes the one and only vehicle to spoon those classic toppings of iceberg, tomato, and the Golden Arches Sauce, of course.

1 pound lean ground beef

Kosher salt and freshly ground black pepper

8 taco-size flour tortillas

8 slices American cheese

½ cup dill pickle slices

1 cup shredded iceberg lettuce

½ cup diced Roma tomato

½ cup diced sweet onion

Golden Arches Sauce (page 259), for serving

PREP
15 minutes

COOK
15 minutes

MAKES
8 tacos

● Heat a large cast-iron or nonstick skillet over medium-high heat. Divide the beef into 8 equal portions and shape into balls. Season each with salt and pepper.

● Press a beef ball onto each tortilla into a patty shape. Place 2 tortillas meat-side down in the skillet and cook until browned and the edges of the beef are crispy, 4 to 5 minutes. Flip the tortilla, add a piece of American cheese on top of the beef, and toast on the other side, another 2 minutes.

● Repeat with the remaining beef, tortillas, and cheese. Top with pickle slices, iceberg lettuce, tomato, sweet onion, and a drizzle of Golden Arches Sauce. Serve.

Mac Daddy Smash Tacos

For all you egg salad haters out there, this one's dedicated to you with all my love. I dare you to try it—you may be converted. It's packed full of fresh herbs, and the gooey yolks make the sauce extra decadent. For the grand finale, it's piled on top of pillowy milk bread. You'll be dreaming of this one all night long.

8 large eggs

⅓ cup Kewpie mayonnaise

1 tablespoon rice vinegar

1 tablespoon sweet relish

1 tablespoon capers, drained and chopped

1 tablespoon Sweet & Spicy Chili Crunch (page 257), drained of excess oil

2 tablespoons chopped fresh parsley

Grated zest of ½ lemon

Kosher salt and freshly ground black pepper

8 slices Japanese milk bread or fluffy white bread

PREP
15 minutes

COOK
8 minutes

MAKES
4 sandwiches

● Bring a medium saucepan of water to a boil. Add the eggs and cook for 8 minutes. While the eggs are cooking, prepare an ice bath next to the stove.

● When the eggs have finished cooking, carefully place them into the ice water using a slotted spoon and cool for 3 minutes. Peel and roughly chop the eggs.

● In a large bowl, combine the chopped eggs, mayonnaise, vinegar, sweet relish, capers, chili crunch, parsley, and lemon zest. Season with salt and pepper to taste and stir to combine. Be careful not to stir too much; you want the egg pieces to remain intact.

● Evenly spoon ½ cup of the egg mixture onto each of 4 slices of the milk bread and top with the second slice. Cut in half and serve.

● Store any leftover egg salad in an airtight container in the fridge for up to 3 days. Serve on fresh bread.

Make It Nice

Swap the mayonnaise for low-fat mayonnaise or 2% Greek yogurt, if you like a tang. Serve open-faced on toasted whole wheat sourdough bread with tomato slices.

Chili Crunch Egg Salad Sandos

You all know I love a Caesar salad. It should be its own food group. It's the pinnacle of cheesy, salty, umami flavors in each bite dressed on cold crunchy lettuce—utter perfection. But what happens when you cross a Caesar salad with a chicken cutlet sandwich? Pure, ridiculous bliss. You get an equal ratio of toasted bread, crunchy chicken, and Caesar-y salad that makes me salivate just even thinking about it.

Crispy Chicken

Canola oil, for frying

1 cup all-purpose flour

2 large eggs, beaten

1 cup panko bread crumbs

½ cup freshly grated Parmesan cheese

1 teaspoon dried thyme

Kosher salt and freshly ground black pepper

4 thin-sliced chicken breast cutlets

Caesar Sandwiches

8 tablespoons extra-virgin olive oil

8 slices sourdough bread

4 cups thinly sliced romaine lettuce

Caesar Dressing (page 113)

Kosher salt and freshly ground black pepper

½ cup shaved Parmesan cheese

PREP
20 minutes

COOK
20 minutes

MAKES
4 sandwiches

● **Make the crispy chicken:** Set a wire rack in a sheet pan and have near the stove. Pour 1 inch of oil into a large, deep saucepan or a large Dutch oven and heat over medium-high heat to 360°F on a deep-fry thermometer.

● **Set up a dredging station with three shallow bowls:** In the first bowl, add the flour. In the second bowl, add the eggs. In the third bowl, combine the panko, Parmesan, and thyme. Season each bowl with salt and pepper.

● Season the chicken cutlets with salt and pepper on both sides. Dredge in the flour, dip in the egg, and coat in the panko/Parmesan mixture, shaking off any excess after each step.

● When the oil is hot (you can test this by adding a piece of panko to the oil and it should sizzle), add 2 pieces of chicken and fry until golden brown and the chicken registers 165°F on a meat thermometer, 4 to 6 minutes. Remove to the rack and repeat with the remaining chicken. Keep warm.

● **Make the Caesar sandwiches:** In a large skillet, heat 1 tablespoon of the olive oil over medium-low heat. Add 2 slices of bread and toast until golden brown, about 3 minutes. Flip the slices and add another 1 tablespoon olive oil. Toast until golden on the second side, another 3 minutes, and remove to a plate. Repeat with the remaining bread and olive oil.

● In a large bowl, toss the romaine with Caesar dressing to your liking to coat. Season with salt and black pepper to taste.

● Set out 4 pieces of toasted sourdough bread. On each, spread a bit of Ceasar dressing, add a piece of chicken, and top with the Caesar salad and lots of Parmesan shavings. Close with the remaining pieces of toast.

Crispy Chicken Caesar Sandwiches

This is for all the steak and martini girlies and gents. It's one of my most viral sandwiches and for good reason: It takes you to heaven and back in a single bite. And here's the recipe in writing, just for you, a love letter of flavor, if you will. The cherry on top, aka secret ingredient, is caramelized red onions. I love the sweet tanginess they add to the steak sandwich and the pretty purple hue.

Caramelized Red Onions

1 tablespoon extra-virgin olive oil

1 tablespoon unsalted butter

2 red onions, thinly sliced

2 teaspoons agave

Kosher salt

1 tablespoon Worcestershire sauce

Rib-Eye Steaks

2 boneless rib-eye steaks (1 pound each), about 1 inch thick

Kosher salt

2 tablespoons extra-virgin olive oil

2 tablespoons unsalted butter

2 garlic cloves, peeled and whole

1 sprig rosemary

Au Poivre Sauce

2 tablespoons black peppercorns, crushed

1 shallot, minced

2 tablespoons Cognac or brandy

1 cup heavy cream

1 tablespoon cold unsalted butter

Kosher salt

Assembly

Olive oil

1 loaf ciabatta, split lengthwise, cut crosswise into 4 buns

PREP
15 minutes

COOK
20 minutes

MAKES
4 sandwiches

● **Make the caramelized red onions:** In a large skillet, heat the olive oil and butter over medium-low heat. Add the onions and agave and season with salt. Cook until softened and deeply golden in color, about 15 minutes. During the last 5 minutes of cooking, add the Worcestershire sauce. Set aside and keep warm.

● **Cook the rib-eye steaks:** Heat a large cast-iron skillet over medium-high heat. Pat both sides of the steaks very dry with paper towels. Season generously with salt.

● Once the pan is hot, add the oil and swirl to coat the pan. Add the steaks, cooking until deep golden brown and medium-rare or 120°F on a meat thermometer, 3 to 4 minutes per side. Add the butter, garlic cloves, and rosemary during the last 2 minutes of cooking and baste the steak once the butter is melted. Remove the steaks from the pan and allow to rest for 10 minutes.

● **Meanwhile, make the au poivre sauce:** Drain off all but about 1 tablespoon of fat from the pan. Return the pan to medium heat. Add the crushed black peppercorns and shallot and toast until fragrant, a minute or so.

● Turn off the flame, stand back from the pan, and add the Cognac. The Cognac will ignite—allow the flame to extinguish. Return the pan to medium heat and allow the Cognac to reduce by half. Stir in the heavy cream and bring to a simmer. Add the butter and whisk until combined. Season with salt to taste and keep warm.

● **Assemble the sandwiches:** To toast the bread, add a drizzle of olive oil to the cut sides of both halves and then toast under the broiler for 1 to 2 minutes until golden brown. Using half of the au poivre sauce, divide it among the 4 bottom buns of the ciabatta loaves. Slice the steak against the grain a little less than ½ inch thick. Place on the ciabatta and top with caramelized onions. Drizzle with the remaining au poivre sauce and add the top buns. Serve.

Steak Sandwiches au Poivre

This combo is truly Iconic, with a capital I. It's a mash-up that is so simple to make, almost like a double-decker personal pan pizza for one. I went for the meat lover's version for this recipe, but feel free to change up the toppings to your liking.

Garlic Butter

3 tablespoons unsalted butter, at room temperature

3 garlic cloves, minced

¼ teaspoon chopped fresh parsley

¼ teaspoon Italian seasoning

Pinch of kosher salt

Pepperoni Grilled Cheese

4 slices sourdough bread

8 slices large pepperoni or spicy salami

6 slices prosciutto

4 tablespoons marinara sauce

½ cup grated mozzarella cheese

¼ cup freshly grated Parmesan cheese

1 tablespoon hot honey, plus more for garnish

Dried oregano

¼ cup mini pepperonis

PREP
15 minutes

COOK
25 minutes

MAKES
2 sandwiches

• **Make the garlic butter:** In a medium bowl, stir together the butter, garlic, parsley, Italian seasoning, and salt until combined.

• **Make the pepperoni grilled cheese:** Preheat a large nonstick skillet over medium heat. Spread an even layer of the garlic butter on one side of each slice of sourdough bread.

• Place 1 slice of the bread buttered-side down in the preheated skillet. While the bread is toasting, top it with 4 slices large pepperoni, 3 slices prosciutto, 2 tablespoons marinara sauce, 2 tablespoons mozzarella, 1 tablespoon Parmesan, ½ tablespoon hot honey, and a pinch of dried oregano.

• Top it with another piece of sourdough bread with the buttered side facing out. Press down on the sandwich and allow to toast for about 5 minutes, until the bread is golden brown and toasted (you may need to reduce the heat to low).

• Flip the sandwich and on the toasted piece of bread, add 2 tablespoons mozzarella and 1 tablespoon Parmesan. Cover the cheeses with the mini pepperonis. Allow the second side to toast until golden brown, another 5 minutes or so. Remove the sandwich to a baking sheet and repeat to make a second sandwich with the remaining ingredients.

• Preheat the broiler to high. Broil both sandwiches until the cheese on top is bubbling, melted, and golden brown, 2 to 3 minutes (watching carefully, as all broilers vary).

• Garnish with a drizzle of hot honey and serve.

Hot Honey Pepperoni Pizza Grilled Cheese

The smash burger is having a moment and for good reason: It's that b*tch. With crispy and caramelized edges—make it a double decker, and slather with maple bacon onion jam, and she'll win you over in one bite.

2 pounds ground beef
  (I like 85/15)

Kosher salt

2 tablespoons avocado or
  canola oil

8 slices American cheese

Garlic Dijonnaise (page 127)

4 potato hamburger buns,
  lightly toasted

Maple Bacon Onion Jam (recipe
  follows)

½ cup pickled jalapeño slices

PREP
15 minutes

COOK
40 minutes

MAKES
4 burgers

- Heat a large cast-iron skillet over high heat. Divide the beef into 8 equal portions and shape into balls. Season generously on all sides with salt.

- When the pan is hot, add the avocado oil and swirl to coat. Add 4 balls of beef, and using a large metal spatula, press firmly down to smash the burger patties very thin. Allow to cook on the first side until deep golden brown, about 3 minutes.

- Flip the burger patties, top with a slice of American cheese, and cook until the burger patties are browned on the second side and the cheese has melted, about 3 minutes. Remove to a plate and repeat with the remaining beef and cheese.

- Add a schmear of garlic Dijonnaise to the bottom of each bun. Top each bun with 2 burger patties, maple bacon onion jam, and pickled jalapeños. Add another schmear of garlic Dijonnaise to the top bun and sandwich together. Enjoy.

MAPLE BACON ONION JAM

Makes about 1 cup

1 pound bacon, cut into ½-inch pieces
1 large yellow onion, diced
½ cup (packed) light brown sugar
½ cup maple syrup
½ cup freshly brewed black coffee
½ cup apple cider vinegar
½ teaspoon red chile flakes
Kosher salt

- Line a plate with paper towels and have near the stove. In a large skillet, cook the bacon over medium heat until browned and crisp, 7 to 8 minutes. Remove to the paper towels to cool.

- To the bacon fat in the skillet, add the onion, reduce the heat to medium-low, and cook, stirring frequently, until caramelized, about 30 minutes.

- Add the bacon pieces, brown sugar, maple syrup, coffee, vinegar, and chile flakes. Bring the sauce to a simmer over medium-low and reduce until it thickens nicely to coat the back of a spoon, about 30 minutes. Season with salt to taste.

- Store any leftover maple bacon jam in an airtight container in the fridge for up to 4 days.

The Naughty Burger

This is exactly what my friends and I want for lunch during a day at the beach in Miami. Flaky white fish that melts in your mouth, swallowed in a light, crispy fried shell with a hint of beer flavor. Topped with an Old Bay cream sauce to give it an extra blanket of love, it's truly the best meal on a sun-drenched day.

Crispy Fish

Canola oil, for frying

4 thick cod fillets (4 to 6 ounces each)

Kosher salt

1¼ cups all-purpose flour

⅓ cup yellow cornmeal

2 teaspoons garlic powder

2 teaspoons onion powder

2 teaspoons paprika

1 large egg

1 (12-ounce) bottle cold beer (I like a pilsner)

Freshly ground black pepper

Sandwiches

2 tablespoons unsalted butter, plus more as needed

4 brioche buns, split open

Old Bay Cream Sauce (page 267)

2 cups shredded iceberg lettuce

1 large tomato, thinly sliced

⅓ cup bread and butter pickle slices

Lemon wedges, for serving

PREP
15 minutes

COOK
15 minutes

MAKES
4 sandwiches

● **Make the crispy fish:** Set a wire rack in a sheet pan and have near the stove. Pour 2 inches of canola oil into a large heavy-bottomed pot and heat over medium-high heat until 375°F on a deep-fry thermometer.

● Pat the cod fillets very dry with paper towels and season with kosher salt to taste on both sides. Set aside.

● In a large bowl, combine the flour, cornmeal, garlic powder, onion powder, paprika, egg, and cold beer and whisk until a smooth batter forms. Season with 1½ teaspoons kosher salt and pepper to taste.

● Dip the fish fillets two at a time into the batter and fry until the fish is nicely golden brown and cooked through, 4 to 6 minutes. Remove to the wire rack to drain, season again with salt, and repeat with the remaining fish fillets and batter.

● **Assemble the sandwiches:** In a large skillet, heat the butter over medium-low heat. Place half of the buns cut-side down in the pan and cook until golden brown, 2 to 3 minutes. Repeat with the remaining buns, adding more butter as needed.

● Schmear some of the Old Bay cream sauce on the bottom of each bun. Top with a piece of fried fish, lettuce, tomato, and bread and butter pickles. Schmear some Old Bay sauce on the top bun and sandwich together. Serve with lemon wedges.

Crispiest of Fish Sandwiches

This is a two-hands sandwich—one just won't do the trick. I swap out the marinara of a traditional sub for my luscious pistachio basil pesto and a creamy vodka sauce— a truly dynamic duo. Topped with a blanket of mozzarella and Parm, you won't even see the beef meatballs peeking out from underneath. One bite, and you'll be swooning.

Meatballs

1 pound ground beef (85/15)

1 large egg, beaten

3 garlic cloves, grated

½ yellow onion, grated

1 tablespoon Italian seasoning

2 tablespoons chopped fresh parsley

Pinch of red chile flakes

⅓ cup freshly grated Parmesan cheese

½ cup dried bread crumbs

Kosher salt and freshly ground black pepper

2 tablespoons extra-virgin olive oil

Vodka Sauce

2 tablespoons extra-virgin olive oil

½ yellow onion, grated

3 garlic cloves, grated

Kosher salt

1 (6-ounce) can tomato paste

3 tablespoons vodka

1 cup heavy cream

¼ teaspoon Aleppo pepper

⅓ cup freshly grated Parmesan cheese

Subs

4 hoagie rolls, split

1 (8-ounce) ball fresh mozzarella, thinly sliced

1 cup Basil Pistachio Pesto (page 261)

⅓ cup freshly grated Parmesan cheese

PREP
20 minutes

COOK
20 minutes

SERVES
4

RECIPE
CONTINUES

Vodka Pesto Meatball Subs

- **Make the meatballs:** In a large bowl, combine the ground beef, egg, garlic, onion, Italian seasoning, parsley, chile flakes, Parmesan, and bread crumbs. Season with salt and pepper. Scoop and roll into 1½-inch meatballs (about 20 meatballs total).

- In a large skillet, heat the olive oil over medium-high heat. Add the meatballs and sear on all sides until browned and cooked through, 7 to 9 minutes. Remove to a plate and carefully wipe out the skillet.

- **Make the vodka sauce:** Return the large skillet to medium-low heat and add the olive oil. Add the onion and garlic and cook until softened, about 3 minutes. Season with salt to taste.

- Add the tomato paste and cook until caramelized and deeper red in color, about 2 minutes. Remove the skillet from the heat and add the vodka. Stir into the tomato paste and set back over medium heat. Add the heavy cream and ¼ cup water and whisk until smooth and combined. Bring to a simmer over medium heat and add the Aleppo pepper and Parmesan.

- Add the meatballs, stirring to coat in the sauce. Continue to simmer until the sauce has thickened on the meatballs and they are cooked through, 3 to 5 minutes.

- **Make the subs:** Position a rack in the upper third of the oven and preheat the broiler to high.

- Place the hoagie rolls on a baking sheet and toast under the broiler until lightly golden, 2 to 3 minutes. Remove the top rolls from the baking sheet and set aside.

- Evenly spoon the bottom rolls with the meatballs and top with the mozzarella. Broil until the cheese is melted, another 2 to 3 minutes.

- Remove from the oven, spoon the pesto over the top bun and sprinkle the meatballs with Parmesan. Sandwich both halves together and serve.

- Store any leftover meatballs in an airtight container in the fridge for up to 4 days. When ready to serve, reheat the meatballs and assemble the sandwich according to the recipe.

Oh, fish tacos, the amount of adoration I have for you is truly limitless. No matter the time of day, place, or occasion, you always make me feel pure joy, like I could be on vacation at the beach even during the middle of a workday. These tacos are loaded with flavor, and the fish is coated in a spicy blackened seasoning that puts the HOT in hot. I add a pineapple salsa on top to cool things down, plus give a refreshing sweetness.

Pineapple Salsa

2 cups finely diced fresh pineapple

¼ cup minced red onion

2 tablespoons chopped fresh cilantro

Juice of 1 lime

1 teaspoon agave

½ teaspoon chili powder

Kosher salt

Avocado Crema

1 avocado, halved and pitted

½ cup sour cream

Juice of 1 lime

¼ teaspoon ground cumin

1 garlic clove, grated

1 teaspoon agave

Kosher salt

Blackened Mahi Mahi

1½ teaspoons paprika

1 teaspoon onion powder

1 teaspoon kosher salt

1 teaspoon garlic powder

½ teaspoon dried oregano

1 teaspoon freshly ground black pepper

4 mahi mahi fillets or thick white fish (4 ounces each)

2 tablespoons avocado or canola oil

Assembly

8 taco-size corn or flour tortillas, warmed

2 cups shredded red cabbage

¼ cup fresh cilantro leaves

Lime wedges, for squeezing

PREP
20 minutes

COOK
15 minutes

MAKES
8 tacos

RECIPE
CONTINUES

Blackened Mahi Tacos with Pineapple Salsa

- **Make the pineapple salsa:** In a medium bowl, toss together the pineapple, red onion, cilantro, lime juice, agave, and chili powder. Season with salt to taste. Set aside to marinate while you cook the tacos.

- **Make the avocado crema:** Scoop the avocado flesh into a food processor. Add the sour cream, lime juice, cumin, garlic, agave, and salt to taste. Pulse until very smooth, scraping down the sides as needed. Add water by the tablespoon until it's easy to drizzle. Set aside.

- **Make the blackened mahi mahi:** In a medium bowl, combine the paprika, onion powder, salt, garlic powder, oregano, and black pepper and mix to combine. Pat the fish very dry on both sides with paper towels.

- In a large cast-iron skillet, heat the avocado oil over medium-high heat. Dredge 2 fish fillets on both sides in the blackened seasoning and place in the pan. Cook until deeply golden and the fish is cooked through and opaque, about 3 minutes per side. Remove to a plate and repeat with the remaining fish fillets.

- **Assemble the tacos:** Cut the fish fillets in half. Add a piece to each tortilla. Top with red cabbage, pineapple salsa, avocado crema, and cilantro. Serve with lime wedges.

Make It Nice

While the blackened fish is already nice, if you prefer less spice, you can also grill the fish without the blackened spice for a delicious and simple charred flavor.

Can I get a hand raised for all those New York–style deli lovers out there? An NYC deli is like a long-distance relationship for me; I fantasize about them from time to time, wish I could call them over for a dinner date, and end up re-creating the memories at home in my kitchen. Call me crazy, but a tuna melt is often my go-to order when the deli and I reunite. It's just comforting love; I add a special hint of sweetness with dried cranberries and apples. I can assure you that you'll want to make a full batch of this tuna salad to have on hand for sandwiches throughout the week.

Tuna Salad

½ cup mayonnaise

Grated zest and juice of
   ½ lemon

4 (5-ounce) cans tuna packed in
   water, drained

1 celery stalk, minced

2 tablespoons sweet pickle
   relish

1 shallot, minced

2 tablespoons chopped fresh
   parsley

1 tablespoon chopped fresh dill

2 tablespoons dried
   cranberries, chopped

1½ teaspoons honey

Kosher salt and freshly ground
   black pepper

Sandwich Melts

4 tablespoons (2 ounces)
   unsalted butter, at room
   temperature

8 slices sourdough bread

8 slices cheddar cheese

1 small Honeycrisp apple, thinly
   sliced into half-moons on a
   mandoline

1 large tomato, thinly sliced

PREP
20 minutes

COOK
10 minutes

MAKES
4
sandwiches

● **Make the tuna salad:** In a large bowl, mix together the mayonnaise, lemon zest, lemon juice, tuna, celery, pickle relish, shallot, parsley, dill, cranberries, and honey and mix to combine. Season with salt and pepper to taste and set aside.

● **Make the sandwich melts:** Heat a large nonstick skillet over low heat. Butter one side of all of the slices of bread. Place 2 slices into the pan buttered-side down, top each with 1 slice of cheddar, some apple slices, one-quarter of the tuna salad, a slice of tomato, and another slice of cheddar. Place the second piece of bread on top, buttered-side up.

● Allow the first side of the sandwich to cook until golden brown, 3 to 4 minutes. Flip, cover the pan with a lid, and let the second side cook until the bread is golden, the cheese is melted, and the tuna is warm, another 3 to 4 minutes. Remove from the pan, slice in half, and serve. Repeat with the remaining sandwich ingredients.

● Store any leftover tuna salad in an airtight container in the fridge for up to 4 days. This makes it easy to assemble sandwiches throughout the week (or just eat it by the spoonful!).

Make It Nice

Substitute Greek yogurt for the mayonnaise in the tuna salad. Make the sandwich into an open-faced melt with 1 slice of bread and 1 slice of cheese. Instead of cooking it in a skillet, toast the bread, shingle over apple slices, and spread with tuna salad. Top with a slice of tomato and cheddar on top. Bake at 350°F until the cheese has melted and the tuna is warmed through, about 8 minutes.

Deli-Style Tuna Melts

There's something about a club sandwich . . . it's a sacred classic. When a club arrives at the table, it towers with delight and brings that pinkies-up moment that no other sandwich can truly rival. This is a club sandwich that got dressed up in a flaky croissant. She's ready for the ball with her newly adorned buttery grown and will impress at any brunch or lunch soirée.

8 slices prosciutto

4 croissants, split horizontally

½ cup Naughty Sauce (page 259)

8 slices ham

8 slices turkey

8 slices cheddar cheese

12 thin slices Roma tomato

Freshly cracked black pepper

2 avocados, thinly sliced

4 romaine lettuce leaves

4 extra-long toothpicks

PREP
15 minutes

COOK
6 minutes

MAKES
4 sandwiches

● Line a plate with paper towels and have near the stove. In a large nonstick pan, cook the prosciutto over medium-low heat until golden and crispy, 2 to 3 minutes per side. Remove to the paper towels to cool; it will continue to crisp.

● On the bottom half of each croissant, spread 2 tablespoons of Naughty Sauce and top with 2 slices ham, 2 slices turkey, 2 slices prosciutto, 2 slices cheddar, 3 slices tomato, some freshly cracked black pepper, thin slices of ½ an avocado, and 1 romaine lettuce leaf. Add the top half of the croissant and secure with a toothpick.

The Croissant Club

Let me begin by saying, this is the ultimate, greatest, and best way to cook chicken thighs for a crowd or to meal-prep for the week. It's a grand statement, but it's true. The chicken gets a nice caramelized outside with a tender, juicy inside that will never make chicken feel boring again. How do I do it? I mimic an actual kebab spit using skewers in the oven with a creamy Greek yogurt marinade that naturally tenderizes the chicken before it roasts.

Marinated Chicken

12 boneless, skinless chicken thighs (about 2¼ pounds total)

¼ cup extra-virgin olive oil

1 cup whole-milk Greek yogurt

6 garlic cloves, minced

Grated zest of 1 lemon

1½ teaspoons kosher salt

1 teaspoon dried oregano

1 teaspoon paprika

1 teaspoon ground cumin

1 teaspoon ground coriander

¼ teaspoon ground cinnamon

1 large yellow onion, peeled

Long, sturdy 10-inch wooden skewers, soaked in water

Assembly

6 pitas, warmed

Silky Smooth Hummus (page 189)

2 cups thinly sliced romaine lettuce

1 cup cherry tomatoes, halved

½ cup thinly sliced pepperoncini peppers

Tzatziki (page 189)

PREP
15 minutes, plus marinating time

COOK
2 hours

MAKES
6 gyros

● **Marinate the chicken:** In a large bowl, combine the chicken thighs, olive oil, yogurt, garlic, lemon zest, salt, oregano, paprika, cumin, coriander, and cinnamon and mix well. Cover and marinate the chicken in the fridge for at least 1 hour and up to overnight.

● Once the chicken is marinated, cut the top and bottom off of the yellow onion to make a thick, flat disc. Place the onion on a surface and insert two skewers into the onion so that they're standing vertically. Stack the pieces of chicken on the skewers like a spit and trim the skewers as needed.

● Remove the top oven rack and position the lower rack in the bottom third of the oven. Preheat the oven to 400°F.

● Line a sheet pan with foil and place a wire rack on top. Place the onion with the skewered chicken onto the rack and add ½ cup water to the bottom of the sheet pan.

● Bake until caramelized on the outside, golden brown, and the chicken registers 165°F on a meat thermometer, 1½ to 2 hours. Add more water to the bottom of the baking sheet throughout the roasting as it evaporates. If the skewered chicken falls over, it's fine, just reposition the chicken standing upright again. Thinly slice the chicken off the skewers into pieces.

● **Assemble the gyros:** In each warmed pita, spread a nice layer of hummus and top with chicken, romaine, cherry tomatoes, pepperoncini, and a drizzle of tzatziki.

● For meal-prepping or leftovers, store the chicken in an airtight container in the fridge for up to 3 days. Store the sandwich toppings in separate containers as well. Reheat the chicken in the microwave or in the oven at 350°F for 5 to 10 minutes until warmed through. Build a sandwich as desired.

Make It Nice

Turn it into a salad. Serve the marinated chicken and gyro toppings over a bed of chopped romaine lettuce for a delicious Greek salad.

Juicy Lemon Chicken Gyros

SEND ME YOUR NOODS

This pasta is inspired by the Amalfi Coast, the land of lemons. It's simple in flavor but unbelievably rich and comforting, yet light. It's the perfect second-date-night pasta to surely win over your latest crush or to serve to friends and family for a night of dinner-table travel. The whipped lemon ricotta creates this silky, creamy sauce when married with the hot bucatini for a pasta twirl that's tough to resist.

Whipped Lemon Ricotta

Grated zest and juice of 1 lemon

8 ounces whole-milk ricotta cheese

Kosher salt and freshly ground black pepper

Lemon Pasta

Kosher salt

1 pound bucatini

2 tablespoons extra-virgin olive oil

3 garlic cloves, thinly sliced

1 shallot, minced

½ teaspoon red chile flakes

Grated zest and juice of 2 lemons

2 tablespoons unsalted butter

½ cup freshly grated Pecorino Romano cheese (2 ounces)

For Serving

Grated lemon zest

2 tablespoons chopped fresh parsley

Freshly cracked black pepper

PREP
15 minutes

COOK
15 minutes

SERVES
4

● **Make the whipped lemon ricotta:** In a food processor, combine the lemon zest, lemon juice, and ricotta. Blend until smooth and creamy. Season to taste with salt and pepper. Remove to a large bowl and set aside.

● **Make the lemon pasta:** Bring a large pot of salted water to a boil. Add the bucatini and cook according to the package directions for al dente. Reserving ½ cup of the pasta cooking water, drain the bucatini and set aside.

● Meanwhile, in a large skillet, heat the olive oil over medium heat. Add the garlic and shallot and cook until translucent and fragrant, about 3 minutes. Add the chile flakes and season with 1 teaspoon salt.

● Add the lemon zest, lemon juice, and butter and stir to combine. Pour into the large bowl with the whipped ricotta.

● Transfer the bucatini to the large bowl with the whipped ricotta. Toss everything together while slowly adding in the pasta water to create a silky, thick sauce. You may not need all of the pasta water; start with half and add more as needed. Sprinkle with the Pecorino Romano and toss again to combine.

● **To serve:** Place the pasta on a large platter and top with some lemon zest, the parsley, and lots of cracked black pepper. Serve immediately.

Lemon Ricotta Pasta

When it comes to lasagna, I love it super saucy with LOTS of layers. So, may I introduce the lasagna pinwheel. You roll the tomato and sausage filling up in the noodle, lay the rolls on their sides, and bake them underneath a luscious, oozy Parmesan cream sauce. The rolled pinwheels add even more filling, sauce, and pasta layers to make the perfect bite—lasagna in its peak, decadent form.

Spicy Sausage Sauce

2 tablespoons extra-virgin olive oil

1 pound hot Italian sausage, casings removed

1 yellow onion, finely diced

3 garlic cloves, thinly sliced

1 teaspoon kosher salt, plus more to taste

½ teaspoon freshly ground black pepper, plus more to taste

1 (6-ounce) can tomato paste

⅔ cup dry white wine

2 teaspoons Italian seasoning

2 teaspoons agave

1 (28-ounce) can crushed tomatoes

Béchamel Sauce

6 tablespoons (3 ounces) unsalted butter

6 tablespoons all-purpose flour

2 cups whole milk

Kosher salt and freshly ground black pepper

½ teaspoon freshly grated nutmeg

¾ cup freshly grated Parmesan cheese

Assembly

Kosher salt

1 pound lasagna noodles

Extra-virgin olive oil

1¼ cups grated mozzarella cheese

Torn fresh basil leaves, for garnish

PREP
25 minutes

COOK
40 minutes

SERVES
6

RECIPE CONTINUES

Baked Lasagna Pinwheels

● **Make the spicy sausage sauce:** In a large high-sided sauté pan, heat the olive oil over medium-high heat. Add the sausage and allow to brown for 2 minutes without moving. Then break the sausage up into crumbles using the back of a wooden spoon or a potato masher. Continue to brown until crumbled and cooked through, another 6 to 7 minutes.

● Add the onion and cook, stirring frequently, until translucent and softened, another 5 minutes. Add the garlic during the last minute or so and season with the salt and pepper.

● Add the tomato paste and stir well until deep red and slightly caramelized, about 3 minutes. Deglaze the pan with the white wine, scraping up any browned bits from the bottom of the pan. Allow to cook and reduce by half.

● Add the Italian seasoning, agave, and crushed tomatoes and stir to combine. Bring to a simmer over medium heat and cook, stirring occasionally, until thickened and the flavors have melded, 12 to 15 minutes. Season with more salt and pepper to taste as desired.

● **Make the béchamel sauce:** In a large saucepan, melt the butter over medium heat. Sprinkle over the flour and whisk until a paste forms. Let the paste cook for a minute or so to cook out the flour flavor. While whisking, slowly stream in the milk, continuing to whisk until smooth. Season with salt and pepper.

● Bring to a simmer and allow to thicken until it nicely coats the back of a spoon, 4 to 6 minutes. Remove from the heat and add the nutmeg and Parmesan, stirring until fully melted. Set aside.

● **To assemble:** Bring a large pot of salted water to a boil. Add the lasagna noodles and cook according to the package directions for al dente.

● Drain the noodles and rinse under cold water to stop the cooking. Separate the noodles onto a baking sheet and lightly drizzle with a little bit of olive oil to keep them from sticking.

● Preheat the oven to 400°F.

● Lightly grease a 2½-quart (or 11 × 7-inch) baking dish with olive oil and set aside. Spread about one-third of the spicy sausage sauce over the base of the dish.

● Onto each lasagna noodle, add a couple of spoonfuls of the spicy sausage sauce down the center. Roll each noodle up and place it on its side, seam-side down, in the baking dish. You should use about a third of the spicy sausage sauce to fill all of the rolled noodles.

● Spoon the last third of the spicy sausage sauce on top of all of the rolled noodles. Evenly spread on the béchamel sauce and top with the grated mozzarella.

● Bake uncovered until bubbling and lightly golden on top, about 25 minutes. If desired, turn the broiler to high and broil until deeply golden brown, 2 to 3 minutes. Allow the lasagna to rest for 10 minutes before serving. Garnish with torn basil.

Let me express my true love for instant ramen noodles. Their curly shape adheres to any delicious sauce in the best of ways to make for the ultimate puckery, slurpy noodle experience. This rib eye noodle stir-fry has a glossy soy-based sauce with hints of ginger and a punch of spice. Paired with melt-in-your-mouth rib eye, it's truly a perfect match.

Sauce and Marinated Rib Eye

½ cup tamari

1 cup beef stock

2 teaspoons toasted sesame oil

2 teaspoons fish sauce

1 tablespoon Sweet & Spicy Chili Crunch (page 257)

3 tablespoons rice vinegar

2 tablespoons light brown sugar

2 tablespoons cornstarch

¾-pound boneless rib eye steak, 1 inch thick, cut into ¼-inch-thick slices

Ramen Noodles

Kosher salt

2 (3-ounce) packages instant ramen noodles, flavor packets discarded

2 tablespoons avocado or canola oil

1 small yellow onion, diced

2 garlic cloves, minced

3 scallions, minced

1 (1-inch) piece fresh ginger, peeled and grated

2 cups sugar snap peas (8 ounces), ends trimmed and halved

2 cups small broccoli florets (6 ounces)

1 red bell pepper, thinly sliced

½ cup baby corn, cut in half

For Serving

1 tablespoon toasted sesame seeds

3 scallions (green part only), thinly sliced

Lime wedges, for squeezing

PREP
25 minutes, plus marinating time

COOK
15 minutes

SERVES
4

RECIPE CONTINUES

Rib Eye Ramen Noodle Stir-Fry

● **Make the sauce and marinate the rib eye:** In a medium bowl, whisk together the tamari, beef stock, sesame oil, fish sauce, chili crunch, vinegar, brown sugar, and cornstarch.

● Divide the marinade in half. Add the steak to half of the marinade in the medium bowl and reserve the remaining sauce on the side for later. Cover and marinate the beef for at least 30 minutes, preferably up to 2 hours in the fridge.

● **Make the ramen noodles:** Bring a large pot of salted water to a boil. Add the ramen noodles and cook for 2 minutes less than the package directions. Drain and rinse under cold water to stop the cooking. Set aside.

● In a large skillet or wok, heat the avocado oil over medium-high heat. Add the marinated steak and cook until browned on both sides, 3 to 4 minutes per side. Remove to a plate and set aside.

● Add the onion and cook, stirring frequently, until softened, about 4 minutes. Add the garlic, scallions, and ginger during the last minute of cooking.

● Add the snap peas, broccoli, red bell pepper, and baby corn and cook until they just begin to soften, 7 to 8 minutes. Season with 1 teaspoon salt. Deglaze with a splash of water to help the veggies steam and cook to crisp-tender.

● Add the reserved sauce, ramen noodles, and beef and toss everything to combine. Bring to a simmer and allow the sauce to reduce and thicken, about 3 minutes.

● **To serve:** Garnish the noodles with toasted sesame seeds and scallion greens and serve with lime wedges for squeezing.

Welcome to decadence at its finest. If you're a French onion lover, may I caution you that this risotto is something you'll want to enjoy in the privacy of your own kitchen. Creamy Arborio rice is cooked until al dente with loads of Gruyère, Parmesan, and, of course, deeply caramelized onions—each spoonful will truly speak to your heart.

Caramelized Onions

2 tablespoons extra-virgin olive oil

2 tablespoons unsalted butter

3 large yellow onions, thinly sliced

1 teaspoon fresh thyme

1 teaspoon kosher salt, plus more to taste

Freshly ground black pepper

Risotto

1 tablespoon extra-virgin olive oil

3 tablespoons unsalted butter

3 garlic cloves, minced

1½ cups Arborio rice

2 teaspoons kosher salt, plus more to taste

¾ cup dry white wine

5 to 6 cups chicken stock, warmed

1½ cups grated Gruyère cheese

½ cup freshly grated Parmesan cheese

2 tablespoons chopped fresh parsley, for garnish

PREP
15 minutes

COOK
1 hour
25 minutes

SERVES
4

● **Make the caramelized onions:** In a large skillet, heat the olive oil and butter over medium-low heat. Add the onions, thyme, salt, and pepper to taste and cook, stirring frequently, until deep golden brown and caramelized, 40 to 50 minutes. If the onions seem like they're burning, deglaze with a splash of water, reduce the heat to low, and continue cooking. Set aside while you make the risotto.

● **Make the risotto:** In a large high-sided sauté pan, heat the olive oil and 1 tablespoon of the butter over medium-low heat. Add the garlic and cook for a minute until fragrant. Add the rice and salt and cook, stirring frequently, until the rice is toasted and slightly translucent in color, about 3 minutes.

● Deglaze the pan with the white wine and bring to a simmer over medium-low heat. Allow to simmer, while constantly stirring, until the wine is almost all evaporated. Ladle in 1 cup of the hot chicken stock at a time, stirring every so often and allowing the stock to simmer and reduce until the stock is nearly all absorbed before adding the next ladle. Repeat this until the rice is al dente and almost all the stock has been used, about 25 minutes. You may not need all of the stock; just be sure the rice is al dente and not too soft.

● Remove the risotto from the heat and stir in the remaining 2 tablespoons butter, the Gruyère, Parmesan, and caramelized onions. Scoop into bowls, garnish with chopped parsley, and serve.

French Onion Risotto

If I tell you to send me noods, this is what I'm talking about. Inspired by the famous Carbone restaurant dish, Spicy Rigatoni Vodka, made right at home, this Calabrian spicy rigatoni is the easiest recipe for the naughtiest of nights. A rich vodka sauce is infused with spicy chiles sopped up by the ridges in the rigatoni for a smoky, sultry experience.

Kosher salt

1 pound rigatoni

2 tablespoons extra-virgin olive oil

1 shallot, minced

4 garlic cloves, minced

1 teaspoon red chile flakes

2 teaspoons chopped Calabrian chili peppers in oil

⅓ cup tomato paste

1 cup heavy cream

½ cup freshly grated Parmesan cheese

½ cup fresh basil leaves, torn

1 (4-ounce) ball burrata

Freshly ground black pepper

PREP
5 minutes

COOK
15 minutes

SERVES
4

● Bring a large pot of heavily salted water to a boil. Add the rigatoni and cook according to the package directions for al dente. Reserving ½ cup of the pasta water, drain the pasta.

● Meanwhile, in a large skillet, heat the olive oil over medium heat. Add the shallot and garlic and cook until softened, 1 to 2 minutes. Add the chile flakes and Calabrian chili peppers and season with a large pinch of salt. Cook for 30 seconds until fragrant.

● Stir in the tomato paste and cook another minute or so, until lightly caramelized. Slowly stream in the heavy cream, stirring constantly to make a smooth sauce. Bring to a simmer over medium heat and allow to cook all together until slightly thickened, another 1 to 2 minutes. Remove from the heat.

● Add the pasta to the skillet and toss to coat, adding dribbles of the pasta water to help the sauce coat the noodles nicely. You may not need all of the reserved pasta water. Add 6 tablespoons of the Parmesan and stir to combine.

● Serve in a large bowl and top with the remaining 2 tablespoons Parmesan, the basil, and a ball of burrata. Grind some fresh pepper all over the top and break open the ball of burrata right before serving.

Calabrian Spicy Rigatoni with Burrata (Obviously)

This pasta will have your eyes rolling to the back of your head. Pillowy gnocchi are tossed in a bath of heavy cream and basil pistachio pesto . . . I mean, what could be better? Topped with melty mozzarella cheese for a cheese pull that'll make your heart skip a beat, it's a crowd-winning recipe that everyone truly loves.

Kosher salt

1 pound store-bought gnocchi

2 teaspoons extra-virgin olive oil

3 garlic cloves, minced

Pinch of red chile flakes

2/3 cup heavy cream

Freshly ground black pepper

1/2 cup grated Parmesan cheese, plus more for garnish

1/2 cup Basil Pistachio Pesto (page 261)

1/2 cup grated mozzarella cheese

2 tablespoons chopped fresh parsley, for garnish

PREP
10 minutes

COOK
40 minutes

SERVES
4

● Bring a large pot of salted water to a boil. Add the gnocchi and cook according to the package directions. Reserving 1/2 cup of the pasta water, drain the gnocchi.

● Meanwhile, in a large high-sided sauté pan, heat the olive oil over medium-low heat. Add the garlic and chile flakes and cook until aromatic, about 30 seconds.

● Add the heavy cream and season with salt and pepper. Bring to a simmer over medium-low heat and allow to reduce until slightly thickened, 3 to 4 minutes. Remove from the heat and stir in the Parmesan and pesto.

● Add the gnocchi and stir to combine, dribbling in a small amount of pasta water as you go to help bind the sauce (you won't need all of the pasta water). Sprinkle with the mozzarella and fold gently until melted.

● Divide among pasta bowls and garnish with more Parmesan and the parsley.

Pesto & Cream Gnocchi

When I'm looking for the pinnacle of comfort foods and the ultimate bite, this short rib ragù is the recipe I turn to every time. The short ribs are seared and then put to bed in a bath of wine and tomato sauce for a 3-hour nap in the oven. This creates melt-in-your-mouth, butter-like meat that is just pure bliss. Tossed with noodles, this is one recipe that is sure to win any crowd over. Apologies in advance if there are no leftovers— this is one of those meat sauces that tastes even better the day after storing in the fridge.

1 tablespoon extra-virgin olive oil

4 pounds bone-in short ribs (9 to 10 ribs)

Kosher salt and freshly ground black pepper

1 medium yellow onion, diced

2 medium carrots, peeled and diced

3 garlic cloves, minced

1½ teaspoons dried thyme

⅓ cup tomato paste

2 cups dry red wine

1 (28-ounce) can crushed tomatoes

1 pound pappardelle pasta or another wide, flat noodle

Freshly grated Parmesan cheese, for serving

PREP
20 minutes

COOK
3 hours
30 minutes

SERVES
6 to 8

- Preheat the oven to 300°F.

- In a large Dutch oven or heavy-bottomed ovenproof pot, heat the olive oil over medium-high heat. Season the short ribs on all sides well with salt and pepper. Working in batches, add the short ribs to the pan and sear on all sides until deep golden brown, 7 to 9 minutes. Remove the short ribs to a plate. Remove all but 2 tablespoons of fat from the pot into a heatproof bowl and set aside to cool and discard.

- Add the onion and carrots to the Dutch oven and cook until softened and translucent, about 3 minutes. Add the garlic and thyme during the last minute of cooking. Add the tomato paste and stir frequently, letting it caramelize and turn deeper red in color, another 2 minutes.

- Deglaze the pot with the red wine, scraping up any of the browned bits from the bottom of the pan. Bring the wine to a simmer over medium-high heat and let reduce for 5 minutes. Season with salt to taste.

- Add the crushed tomatoes and return the seared short ribs to the pot. Bring the whole mixture to a simmer over medium-high heat, then cover the pot and transfer to the oven. Bake until the meat is almost fork-tender, about 2½ hours.

- Uncover and continue to bake for 30 minutes to help the short ribs brown and the sauce to reduce. If the sauce is reducing too much, add a splash of water and stir to combine.

- Transfer the short ribs to a large bowl. Remove and discard the bones and shred the meat, using two forks. Return the meat to the sauce, stir to combine, and taste for seasoning.

- When ready to serve, bring a large pot of salted water to a boil. Add the pappardelle and cook according to the package directions for al dente.

- Reserving ½ cup pasta water, drain the pasta and toss with the short rib ragù, adding dribbles of pasta water as needed to combine. Serve with Parmesan.

- Store any leftover ragù in an airtight container in the fridge for up to 4 days. This sauce also freezes well for up to 2 months. Reheat on the stove until warmed through and toss with freshly boiled pasta.

Short Rib Ragù

Whether you're a mushroom lover or not, this sauce is comfort in a bowl. It's a rich and hearty ragù with hints of wine, tomato, and a dash of cream (of course). A drizzle of truffle oil to finish adds that secret umami flavor at the end that will make you want to keep twirling your fork for more. It's a whole new way to make mushrooms shine.

Kosher salt

1 pound tagliatelle or fettuccine

2 tablespoons unsalted butter

1 tablespoon extra-virgin olive oil, plus more as needed

2½ tablespoons white truffle oil

2 shallots, diced

3 garlic cloves, minced

1 pound hen of the woods (maitake) mushrooms, torn into 1-inch pieces

1 pound Baby Bella mushrooms, torn into 1-inch pieces

1 pound shiitake mushrooms, stemmed and torn into ½-inch pieces

1 tablespoon fresh thyme

½ teaspoon freshly ground black pepper, plus more to taste

¾ cup dry red wine

2 cups canned crushed tomatoes

1 cup vegetable stock

½ cup heavy cream

½ cup freshly grated Parmesan cheese, for serving

2 tablespoons chopped fresh parsley, for garnish

PREP
20 minutes

COOK
38 minutes

SERVES
4

● Bring a large pot of salted water to a boil. Add the tagliatelle and cook according to the package directions for al dente. Reserving ½ cup of the pasta water, drain the pasta.

● Meanwhile, in a large Dutch oven or heavy-bottomed pot, heat the butter, olive oil, and 1 tablespoon of the truffle oil over medium heat. Add the shallots and cook, stirring occasionally, until softened, about 3 minutes. Add the garlic during the last minute of cooking.

● Add the hen of the woods, Baby Bella, and shiitake mushrooms and cook, stirring frequently, until the liquid has released and mushrooms have browned, 10 to 12 minutes, adding a bit more olive oil as needed. Add the thyme and season with 1 teaspoon salt and the pepper.

● Deglaze with the red wine and bring to a simmer. Allow to simmer until the wine has reduced by almost half, 3 to 5 minutes.

● Add the crushed tomatoes and vegetable stock, bring to a simmer, and cook until thickened and the flavors have melded, about 15 minutes.

● Reduce the heat to low and stir in the heavy cream. Taste for additional seasoning and keep warm if the pasta isn't ready yet.

● Add the drained pasta to the mushroom ragù with a couple of dribbles of pasta water to emulsify the sauce. Toss to evenly coat.

● Divide among plates and drizzle with the remaining 1½ tablespoons truffle oil. Sprinkle with the Parmesan and garnish with the parsley.

Truffle Mushroom Ragù

Truffle Mushroom Ragù, page 171

This is the mac and cheese of all mac and cheeses. Cavatappi noodles, with their sultry curves, soak up a sauce made with five types of cheese. Topped with a buttery cracker topping, it's crunchy, creamy, and luscious.

Softened butter, for the baking dish

Cheese Sauce

2 tablespoons unsalted butter

1 shallot, diced

2 garlic cloves, minced

2 tablespoons all-purpose flour

2 cups whole milk

4 ounces cream cheese, at room temperature

2 cups grated sharp yellow cheddar cheese (8 ounces)

1 cup grated Fontina cheese (4 ounces)

1 cup grated Gouda cheese (4 ounces)

1 cup grated Gruyère cheese (4 ounces)

2 teaspoons kosher salt

½ teaspoon freshly ground black pepper

1 teaspoon garlic powder

1 teaspoon onion powder

1 teaspoon mustard powder

1 teaspoon paprika

⅛ teaspoon cayenne pepper

Assembly

Kosher salt

12 ounces cavatappi pasta

2 tablespoons unsalted butter, melted

1 cup finely crushed butter crackers (about 24 crackers)

1 tablespoon chopped fresh parsley

PREP
15 minutes

COOK
28 minutes

SERVES
6 to 8

● Preheat the oven to 350°F. Butter a 9 × 13-inch baking dish and set aside.

● **Make the cheese sauce:** In a large Dutch oven or heavy-bottomed pot, heat the butter over medium heat. Add the shallot and garlic and cook until softened, about 4 minutes. Add the flour and whisk until a paste forms. While whisking, slowly drizzle in the milk and whisk until smooth.

● Bring the milk mixture to a simmer over medium heat and allow to thicken slightly, about 4 minutes.

● Add the cream cheese, cheddar, Fontina, Gouda, and Gruyère. Stir until well combined, smooth, and melted. Season to taste with the salt and pepper. Remove from the heat and add the garlic powder, onion powder, mustard powder, paprika, and cayenne. Set aside and keep warm.

● **To assemble:** Bring a large pot of salted water to a boil. Add the pasta and cook according to the package directions for al dente. Reserving 1 cup of the pasta cooking water, drain the pasta.

● Meanwhile, in a small bowl, combine the melted butter and crushed crackers. Set aside.

● Add the pasta noodles to the cheese sauce with ½ cup of the pasta cooking water and stir to combine, adding more pasta water as needed to make a silky sauce. Transfer the mixture to the prepared baking dish and top with the crushed butter crackers.

● Bake until bubbling and hot, 18 to 20 minutes.

● Serve garnished with the parsley.

Five-Cheese
Mac & Cheese

The queen of them all, the carbonara, adorned in her silky Pecorino sauce and studded with crispy pancetta jewels, rules over any pasta dish. Mine happens to be extra decadent with a dollop of the creamiest stracciatella cheese, and an egg yolk to garnish. This is an extra-special pasta dish when you're ready to impress, thanks to the sexy sauce. Be sure to have plenty of Pecorino Romano to garnish—you'll want to make it rain with cheesy goodness.

Kosher salt

1 pound spaghetti

¾ teaspoon coarsely ground black pepper, plus more for serving

2 large eggs

3 large egg yolks, plus 4 pasteurized egg yolks for garnish

½ cup finely grated Parmesan cheese

¾ cup finely grated Pecorino Romano, plus more for serving

1 tablespoon extra-virgin olive oil

6 ounces cubed pancetta

½ cup stracciatella

PREP
15 minutes

COOK
15 minutes

SERVES
4

- Bring a large pot of salted water to a boil. Add the pasta and cook to 1 minute shy of the package directions for al dente. Reserving 1 cup of the pasta cooking water, drain the pasta.

- Meanwhile, in a large skillet, toast the coarse black pepper over low heat until fragrant. Set aside to cool slightly.

- In a large bowl, whisk together the whole eggs, 3 large egg yolks, Parmesan, and ½ cup of the Pecorino. Season with 1½ teaspoons salt and the toasted black pepper. Set aside.

- In the same large skillet, heat the olive oil over medium heat. Add the pancetta and cook, stirring frequently, until the fat renders and the pancetta is golden brown, 6 to 7 minutes. Remove from the heat and keep warm if the pasta isn't ready yet.

- Add the drained pasta to the skillet with the pancetta and toss to coat for a minute.

- Transfer the hot pasta and pancetta to the large bowl with the egg mixture. Toss to evenly coat, allowing a sauce to form and adding dribbles of the hot pasta water, starting with ¼ cup and adding more as needed to fully emulsify the sauce. The hot noodles will cook the egg to form the creamiest of sauces.

- Divide among four shallow pasta bowls. Top each with a dollop of stracciatella, additional Pecorino Romano, 1 pasteurized egg yolk, and additional black pepper. Serve.

Saucy Carbonara

THE
MAIN
SQUEEZE

Say hello to the salmon bowl of your dreams, similar to a deconstructed sushi bowl, but dare I say better? I cube the salmon and marinate it in a sweet and salty sauce of soy and honey. The marinade transforms into this deliciously sinful glaze that caramelizes onto the salmon when it's cooked. You can thank me when this bowl is on weekly rotation in your meal planning routine.

Honey Soy Salmon

4 garlic cloves, minced

2 teaspoons minced fresh ginger

⅓ cup reduced-sodium soy sauce or tamari

½ teaspoon red chile flakes or Sweet & Spicy Chili Crunch (page 257)

½ teaspoon onion powder

1 teaspoon toasted sesame oil

⅓ cup honey or agave

2 skinless salmon fillets (8 ounces each), cut into 1½-inch pieces

Bowls

1½ cups cooked long-grain white or brown rice

½ English cucumber, thinly sliced

1 avocado, thinly sliced

3 scallions, thinly sliced

4 tablespoons spicy mayonnaise

2 tablespoons Sweet & Spicy Chili Crunch (page 257)

1 (0.35-ounce) package nori seaweed snack sheets, to serve

PREP
15 minutes, plus marinating time

COOK
10 minutes

MAKES
2 or 3 bowls

● **Make the honey soy salmon:** In a medium bowl, combine the garlic, ginger, soy sauce, chile flakes, onion powder, sesame oil, and honey. Add the salmon and toss to fully coat. Place plastic wrap over the top of the bowl and put in the refrigerator to marinate for at least 1 hour and up to 4 hours.

● When ready to cook the salmon, heat a large nonstick skillet over medium-high heat and add the salmon plus the marinade. Cook until the salmon is golden brown and lightly caramelized on one side, about 5 minutes. Flip the salmon cubes and cook until the salmon is opaque, cooked through, and caramelized on both sides, another 5 minutes (the sauce will thicken as well to become a glaze).

● **Assemble the bowls:** Spoon the rice into two or three bowls. Top with the cucumber, avocado, and salmon cubes. Garnish with the scallions, a drizzle of spicy mayonnaise, and the chili crunch, and serve with nori seaweed snack sheets.

Honey Soy Salmon Bowls

I have no words to even describe how much I love these flavors. First up is the skirt steak: It's the most underrated cut of beef that happens to be insanely tender and easy to cook. Marry it with a nice slather of chimichurri full of fresh herb and spice—it's a duo that's truly meant to be. Adding a side of crispy asparagus with a coat of Parmesan truly makes you feel warm and fuzzy on the inside.

Chimichurri

1 shallot, diced

1 red Fresno chile, minced

3 to 4 garlic cloves, minced

½ cup red wine vinegar

1 teaspoon kosher salt

1 teaspoon red chile flakes

½ cup chopped fresh cilantro

¼ cup chopped fresh parsley

1 tablespoon dried oregano

¾ cup extra-virgin olive oil

Parmesan Asparagus

1 pound asparagus, ends trimmed

2 tablespoons extra-virgin olive oil

2 garlic cloves, minced

¼ teaspoon kosher salt

¼ teaspoon freshly ground black pepper

¼ cup finely grated Parmesan cheese

Grated zest of ½ lemon, for sprinkling

Flaky sea salt, for sprinkling

Skirt Steak

1 (1½-pound) skirt steak

Kosher salt and freshly ground black pepper

1 tablespoon extra-virgin olive oil

1 sprig rosemary

1 garlic clove, smashed and peeled

1 tablespoon unsalted butter

Flaky sea salt, for garnish

PREP
20 minutes

COOK
18 minutes

SERVES
4

RECIPE CONTINUES

Skirt Steak with Chimichurri & Parmesan Asparagus

● **Make the chimichurri:** In a small bowl, stir together the shallot, Fresno chile, garlic, vinegar, salt, chile flakes, cilantro, parsley, oregano, and olive oil. Set aside for the flavors to marinate.

● **Make the Parmesan asparagus:** Preheat the oven to 425°F. Line a sheet pan with parchment paper.

● In a large bowl, toss the asparagus with the olive oil, garlic, kosher salt, and pepper. Evenly spread on the baking sheet and top with the Parmesan.

● Bake until the asparagus is just tender and the cheese is lightly golden, about 18 minutes.

● Sprinkle with the lemon zest and some flaky sea salt.

● **Cook the skirt steak:** Let the steak come to room temperature for 30 minutes. Meanwhile, preheat the grill, a grill pan, or a large cast-iron skillet to medium-high heat. Season the steak with salt and pepper.

GRILL METHOD

Drizzle the steak with the olive oil. Cook the steak on the grill on both sides until medium-rare and it registers 125°F on a meat thermometer, 3 to 4 minutes per side. Remove the steak to a plate and let it rest for 10 minutes before slicing and serving.

STOVETOP METHOD

Add the olive oil to the hot skillet or grill pan. Sear the steak for 2 to 3 minutes on the first side until deep golden brown. Flip the steak and add the rosemary, garlic, and butter. Cook the steak for another 2 minutes until deeply golden brown, basting the steak with butter to finish. Remove the steak to a plate and let it rest for 10 minutes before slicing and serving.

● Slice the steak against the grain and serve with a side of asparagus. Drizzle over the chimichurri and serve the remaining in a bowl on the side.

● Store any extra chimichurri in an airtight container in the fridge for up to 3 days.

Curry is one of my favorite feel-good foods. It's velvety, rich, and bursting with bright flavors in every bite. I love adding perfectly cooked shrimp to the coconutty sauce that's scented with a hint of fish sauce, cilantro, and a spoonful of brown sugar for sweetness.

Shrimp

1 tablespoon avocado oil or canola oil

1 pound peeled and deveined large shrimp

1 teaspoon reduced-sodium soy sauce or tamari

½ teaspoon red chile flakes

2 garlic cloves, minced

Kosher salt

Curry

1 tablespoon avocado oil

1 medium yellow onion, thinly sliced

1 red bell pepper, thinly sliced

1 cup sugar snap peas, ends trimmed and cut in half

3 heads baby bok choy, roughly chopped

4 garlic cloves, minced

1 (1-inch) piece fresh ginger, peeled and grated

3 tablespoons red curry paste

½ cup chicken or vegetable broth

1 tablespoon light brown sugar

2 tablespoons reduced-sodium soy sauce or tamari

1 tablespoon fish sauce

1 tablespoon unsalted butter

1 (15-ounce) can full-fat coconut milk, well shaken

Juice of 1 lime

For Serving

2 cups cooked jasmine rice

Sriracha

Fresh cilantro leaves

Fresh Thai basil or basil leaves

Lime wedges, for squeezing

PREP
15 minutes

COOK
15 minutes

SERVES
4

RECIPE CONTINUES

Thai Coconut Curry with Shrimp

- **Cook the shrimp:** In a large skillet, heat the avocado oil over medium-high heat. In a medium bowl, toss the shrimp with the soy sauce, chile flakes, and garlic. Season with salt to taste.

- Add the shrimp to the skillet and cook on both sides until lightly golden brown and opaque, 2 to 3 minutes per side. Remove to a plate and set aside.

- **Make the curry:** Return the skillet to medium-high heat, adding the avocado oil. Add the onion, bell pepper, snap peas, and bok choy and cook until almost tender, about 4 minutes. Add the garlic, ginger, and red curry paste. Allow to cook until fragrant, about 1 minute.

- Deglaze the skillet with the chicken broth, scraping up the browned bits from the bottom of the pan. Add the brown sugar, soy sauce, fish sauce, and butter. Whisk until smooth and combined. While whisking, add the coconut milk. Add the shrimp and simmer until the flavors meld and the shrimp are coated nicely in the sauce, 1 to 2 minutes. Drizzle with the lime juice.

- **To serve:** Serve over rice and garnish with sriracha, cilantro, and basil, with lime wedges on the side for squeezing.

Scrap Abba's man after midnight. *This* is what I want at half past twelve. It's also my ultimate lunch or dinner, especially when it comes to meal-prepping. Make all of the toppings in advance and assemble a colorful bowl with the creamiest hummus for the freshest of flavors in each bite.

Greek-Spiced Chicken

1 pound chicken breast tenders

2 tablespoons extra-virgin olive oil

Grated zest of ½ lemon

Juice of 1 lemon

1 teaspoon dried oregano

1 teaspoon ground cumin

½ teaspoon ground coriander

Kosher salt and freshly ground black pepper

Bowls

Silky Smooth Hummus (recipe follows)

2 cups cooked jasmine rice

1 cup cherry tomatoes, diced

¼ cup pitted kalamata olives, chopped

Too Easy Pickled Red Onions (page 265)

2 Persian (mini) cucumbers, thinly sliced into half moons

½ teaspoon dried oregano

¼ cup chopped fresh dill

½ cup crumbled feta cheese (2 ounces)

Tzatziki (recipe follows)

PREP
25 minutes

COOK
15 minutes

SERVES
4

● **Make the Greek-spiced chicken:** In a large bowl or zip-top bag, combine the chicken tenders, olive oil, lemon zest, lemon juice, oregano, cumin, coriander, and salt and pepper to taste. Allow to marinate while you prep the rest of the recipe, but if possible, marinate for 1 to 2 hours in the fridge.

● When ready to cook, heat a grill, grill pan, or cast-iron skillet to medium-high heat. Alternatively, preheat the oven to 350°F and line a sheet pan with parchment paper.

GRILL OR STOVETOP METHOD

Remove the chicken tenders from the marinade and cook on both sides until golden brown and a meat thermometer registers 165°F, about 3 minutes per side. Cut into bite-size pieces and keep warm.

OVEN METHOD

Place the chicken tenders on the baking sheet and roast until golden brown and 165°F on a meat thermometer, about 25 minutes. Remove to a plate, cut into bite-size pieces, and keep warm until ready to serve.

● **Assemble the bowls:** Divide the hummus among four shallow bowls. In piles, top with rice, cherry tomatoes, olives, pickled onions, cucumbers, oregano, and the Greek-spiced chicken. Sprinkle with dill and feta, and drizzle with tzatziki to finish.

● For any leftovers or when meal-prepping, store all of the components in different airtight containers in the fridge for up to 3 days. Build individual bowls when ready to serve.

Gimme Gimme Gimme a Greek Island Bowl

SILKY SMOOTH HUMMUS

Makes 1½ cups

1 (15.5-ounce) can chickpeas, drained and rinsed
1 garlic clove, peeled but whole
½ teaspoon ground cumin
½ teaspoon smoked paprika
⅓ cup tahini
Juice of 1 lemon
⅓ cup extra-virgin olive oil
Kosher salt and freshly ground black pepper

● In a medium saucepan, combine the chickpeas and 2 cups water and bring to a boil over medium-high heat. Cook until lightly softened, about 5 minutes. Reserving ⅓ cup of the cooking liquid, drain the chickpeas and place in a food processor.

● Add the garlic, cumin, smoked paprika, tahini, lemon juice, hot cooking liquid, and olive oil and blend until smooth and whipped to a light and silky consistency. Season with salt and pepper to taste. The hummus can be stored in an airtight container in the refrigerator for up to 1 week.

TZATZIKI

Makes 1½ cups

1 cup whole-milk Greek yogurt
½ English cucumber, grated (about ½ cup)
Juice of 1 lemon
1 garlic clove, grated
1 tablespoon chopped fresh dill
1 tablespoon chopped fresh mint leaves (optional)
Kosher salt

● In a medium bowl, stir together the yogurt, cucumber, lemon juice, garlic, dill, mint (if using), and salt to taste. Refrigerate until ready to serve.

This is one of those ideas that may have just come to me one late night when all I dreamed of was to somehow get a Double-Double cheeseburger delivered from In-N-Out to Miami. I couldn't stop salivating at the thought of it. Instead, this quesadilla was born, and now it's a staple late-night snack for my friends to soak up any boozy beverages we might have been drinking.

Double-Double Spread

- ½ cup mayonnaise, light or regular
- 3 tablespoons ketchup
- 1 teaspoon yellow mustard
- 1 teaspoon distilled white vinegar
- 2½ tablespoons sweet pickle relish
- Kosher salt and freshly ground black pepper

Cheeseburger Mixture

- 2 tablespoons extra-virgin olive oil
- 1 pound ground beef (85/15)
- Kosher salt
- 1 medium yellow onion, diced
- 2 garlic cloves, grated
- 1 teaspoon paprika
- 1 teaspoon onion powder
- ¼ cup ketchup
- 1 tablespoon Dijon mustard

Quesadillas

- 4 extra-large burrito-size flour tortillas
- 2 cups shredded Mexican cheese blend
- ⅓ cup minced yellow onion
- ⅓ cup minced dill pickles
- 4 slices bacon, cooked and crumbled
- Cooking spray, for the pan
- 2 cups thinly sliced iceberg lettuce
- 2 Roma tomatoes, diced

PREP
15 minutes

COOK
20 minutes

SERVES
4

RECIPE
CONTINUES

Double-Double Cheeseburger Quesadillas

● **Make the double-double spread:** In a small bowl, combine the mayonnaise, ketchup, yellow mustard, vinegar, sweet pickle relish, and a pinch of salt and pepper. Set aside until ready to serve.

● **Make the cheeseburger mixture:** In a large skillet, heat the olive oil over medium heat. Add the ground beef and cook until browned and crumbled, 6 to 7 minutes. Season with salt to taste.

● Add the onion and cook until translucent and tender, another 3 to 4 minutes. Add the garlic, paprika, onion powder, ketchup, and mustard. Stir to combine, allowing to warm through, and set aside.

● **Make the quesadillas:** Set a tortilla on the work surface and sprinkle with ½ cup cheese, one-quarter of the cheeseburger mixture, onion, pickles, and bacon. Fold into a half-moon shape.

● Heat a large nonstick skillet over medium-low heat. Lightly grease the preheated pan with cooking spray. Add the quesadilla and cook on both sides until golden brown and the cheese has melted, 3 minutes per side.

● Remove from the heat. Quickly peel open the quesadilla and add some of the iceberg lettuce and tomato. Cut in half and serve with the double-double spread. Repeat to make a total of 4 quesadillas.

Oh, chicken Parm, I could write you a love letter any day of the week. You're juicy yet crispy, dressed in a blanket of sauce and mozz that's hard to deny. One bite, and you keep my mouth watering. While your classic recipe is solid to its core, I love to dress you up in vodka sauce as a twist.

Vodka Sauce

2 tablespoons extra-virgin olive oil

1 large shallot, minced

½ small yellow onion, finely chopped

3 garlic cloves, minced

½ teaspoon red chile flakes

1 (6-ounce) can tomato paste

3 tablespoons vodka

1 cup heavy cream

1½ teaspoons agave

2 tablespoons unsalted butter

Kosher salt and freshly ground black pepper

⅓ cup freshly grated Parmesan cheese

Chicken

2 boneless, skinless chicken breasts (8 ounces each)

Kosher salt and freshly ground black pepper

1 cup all-purpose flour

3 large eggs, beaten

2 cups panko bread crumbs

½ cup freshly grated Parmesan cheese

2 teaspoons Italian seasoning

Assembly

Canola oil, for frying

8 ounces fresh mozzarella, thinly sliced

½ cup freshly grated Parmesan cheese

Torn fresh basil, for garnish

PREP
20 minutes

COOK
25 minutes

SERVES
4

RECIPE
CONTINUES

Epic Chicken Vodka Parm

● **Make the vodka sauce:** In a large heavy-bottomed pot, heat the olive oil over medium heat. Add the shallot, onion, and garlic and cook until softened, 3 to 4 minutes.

● Add the chile flakes and tomato paste and cook until the tomato paste deepens in color, about 2 minutes. Remove the pan quickly from the heat and deglaze with the vodka. Stir until the vodka evaporates and return the pan to the burner over medium heat. Be careful: If the vodka ignites, remove the pan from the heat and let the flames die.

● Stir in the heavy cream, agave, and butter and season with salt and pepper to taste. Remove from the heat and stir in the Parmesan. The sauce should be on the thicker side. If it's too thick, simply add ¼ cup hot water and stir. Set aside and keep warm.

● **Prepare the chicken:** Slice each chicken breast in half horizontally to make 4 cutlets. Place one chicken breast in between two pieces of plastic wrap. Pound the chicken using a meat mallet until it's about ¼ inch thick. Repeat with the remaining pieces of chicken and season on both sides with salt and pepper.

● **Set up a dredging station with three shallow bowls:** Add the flour to the first bowl. Add the eggs to the second bowl. In the third bowl, combine the panko, Parmesan, and Italian seasoning. Season each bowl well with salt and pepper.

● **To assemble:** Set a wire rack in a sheet pan and have near the stove. In a large high-sided sauté pan, heat ½ inch canola oil over medium-high heat until hot and shimmering.

● Dredge the chicken in the flour, shaking off any excess. Dip in the egg and then dredge in the panko mixture, again shaking off any excess.

● Add 2 chicken cutlets to the hot oil and fry until golden brown and the chicken is cooked through, 2 to 3 minutes per side. Remove the chicken to the wire rack and season with salt. Repeat with the remaining chicken breasts.

● Once all of the chicken has been fried and is sitting on the wire rack, preheat the broiler. Spoon a generous amount of vodka sauce over each piece of chicken. Top with a slice or two of mozzarella.

● Place the sheet pan under the broiler and cook until the cheese is melted and lightly golden, 2 to 3 minutes. Garnish with Parmesan and basil, and serve with extra vodka sauce on the side.

Let's get one thing straight: Fish is never boring. Well, sometimes—but not this time. Just ask my friends, who drop everything to come over for this specific dish whenever I make it. She's dressed up in Parmesan and panko, lathered in a lemon cream sauce, and devoured as quickly as it took to make her. And you can use any fish you like!

Lemon Cream Sauce

2 tablespoons unsalted butter

1 shallot, finely chopped

1 cup dry white wine

1½ cups heavy cream

½ teaspoon agave

1½ teaspoons kosher salt, plus more to taste

Freshly ground black pepper

Juice of 1 lemon, plus more to taste

1 tablespoon Dijon mustard

Parmesan Herb–Crusted Salmon

4 salmon fillets (4 to 5 ounces each)

Kosher salt

½ cup panko bread crumbs

½ cup freshly grated Parmesan cheese

1 teaspoon sweet paprika

Grated zest of 1 lemon

1 tablespoon fresh thyme

1 tablespoon chopped fresh parsley

Freshly ground black pepper

2 tablespoons Dijon mustard

2 tablespoons extra-virgin olive oil

Lemon wedges, for squeezing

PREP
15 minutes

COOK
20 minutes

SERVES
4

● **Make the lemon cream sauce:** In a medium saucepan, heat the butter over medium-high heat. Add the shallot and cook until softened, about 2 minutes. Add the wine and bring to a simmer over medium-high heat. Allow the wine to reduce by three-quarters, about 5 minutes.

● Reduce the heat to medium and whisk in the cream, agave, salt, and pepper to taste. Add the lemon juice and mustard. Simmer over medium-low heat until thickened, 2 to 3 minutes. Adjust the salt, pepper, and lemon juice to taste. Set aside until ready to serve.

● **Make the Parmesan herb–crusted salmon:** Preheat the oven to 375°F. Line a baking sheet with parchment paper.

● Pat the fish fillets dry with paper towels and season on both sides with salt. Set aside.

● In a medium bowl, combine the panko, Parmesan, paprika, lemon zest, thyme, and parsley. Mix to combine and season with salt and pepper.

● Lightly brush the salmon fillets with the mustard and top with the panko/Parmesan mixture, pressing down lightly to adhere. Place on the prepared baking sheet and drizzle the tops with the olive oil.

● Bake until golden brown and the fish is opaque, 13 to 15 minutes.

● Serve with the lemon cream sauce and lemon wedges.

Parmesan Herb–Crusted Salmon

Ready to cook to impress? This is your dish. Whether it's for family and friends, a new date, or by yourself on the couch, I guarantee this chicken will get the kiss of approval. Start with a creamy artichoke dip that's truly spoonable on its own. Stuff it inside seasoned chicken that's seared and baked to perfection. It's moist, juicy, and creamy all in one bite.

Artichoke Dip

2 ounces frozen spinach, thawed

4 ounces cream cheese, at room temperature

¼ cup canned artichoke hearts, drained and chopped

¼ cup grated mozzarella cheese

2 tablespoons freshly grated Parmesan cheese

Grated zest of ½ lemon

2 garlic cloves, grated

Pinch of red chile flakes (optional)

Pinch of freshly grated nutmeg

Kosher salt and freshly ground black pepper

Chicken

4 boneless, skinless chicken breasts (8 ounces each)

Kosher salt and freshly ground black pepper

1 tablespoon Italian seasoning

1 teaspoon garlic powder

1 teaspoon onion powder

1 teaspoon paprika

2 tablespoons extra-virgin olive oil

2 tablespoons chopped fresh parsley, for garnish

PREP
20 minutes

COOK
25 minutes

SERVES
4

- **Make the artichoke dip:** Place the spinach in a clean kitchen towel and wring out the excess liquid. Place in a medium bowl.

- Add the cream cheese, artichoke hearts, mozzarella, Parmesan, lemon zest, garlic, chile flakes, and nutmeg to the spinach. Stir to combine and season with salt and pepper. Divide the dip in half and set aside.

- **Prepare the chicken:** Preheat the oven to 400°F.

- Cut a pocket into each chicken breast by slicing into it horizontally but taking care not to cut all the way through.

- Season all sides of the chicken breasts with salt and pepper. Stuff the inside of each pocket with ¼ cup of the artichoke dip. Reassemble the breasts and secure with one to two toothpicks.

- In a small bowl, combine the Italian seasoning, garlic powder, onion powder, and paprika and sprinkle evenly all over the chicken breasts.

- Heat a large ovenproof skillet over medium-low heat and add the olive oil. Sear the breasts, in batches if needed, until golden brown, 3 to 5 minutes per side.

- Transfer the skillet to the oven and roast until the chicken is fully cooked through and registers 165°F on a meat thermometer, 10 to 15 minutes. Remove from the oven, garnish with parsley, and serve.

Artichoke Dip–Stuffed Chicken

Pull out your candlesticks, white tablecloth, and nicest dishes. It's time to bring your favorite steakhouse right to your dining room table. When it comes to steak night at home, the most important thing is to buy a great piece of meat. I love a good New York strip seared until golden and tender in a cast-iron skillet, then finished in a bath of garlic butter. Served with crisp-tender spiced fingerling potatoes, it's love at first bite.

Garlic Butter

4 tablespoons (2 ounces/ ½ stick) unsalted butter, at room temperature

2 garlic cloves, grated

1 teaspoon fresh thyme

1 tablespoon freshly grated Parmesan cheese

½ teaspoon Italian seasoning

Flaky sea salt

Spiced Roasted Potatoes

1 pound fingerling potatoes, halved lengthwise

2 tablespoons extra-virgin olive oil

2 teaspoons steak seasoning

½ teaspoon paprika

Kosher salt and freshly ground black pepper

Steak

2 New York strip steaks (12 ounces each), about 1 inch thick

Kosher salt and freshly ground black pepper

1 tablespoon extra-virgin olive oil

Flaky sea salt, for garnish

PREP
20 minutes

COOK
35 minutes

SERVES
4

● **Make the garlic butter:** In a small bowl, combine the butter, garlic, thyme, Parmesan, Italian seasoning, and a hearty pinch of flaky sea salt. Mash with a fork until well combined. Place in a piece of plastic wrap and shape into a log. Place into the freezer for 30 minutes to firm up.

● **Make the spiced roasted potatoes:** Preheat the oven to 425°F. Line a baking sheet with parchment paper.

● In a large bowl, toss the potatoes with the olive oil, steak seasoning, paprika, and salt and pepper to taste. Spread evenly on the lined baking sheet.

● Roast until golden brown and tender, 30 to 35 minutes, flipping halfway through. Set aside and keep warm.

● **Cook the steak:** Bring the steaks to room temperature 30 minutes prior to cooking. Pat both sides of the steak very dry with paper towels and season with salt and pepper.

● Heat a large cast-iron skillet over medium-high heat. Add the olive oil and swirl to coat. Add the steaks and cook until deep golden brown on both sides and medium-rare, which is 120° to 125°F on a meat thermometer, 4 to 5 minutes per side.

● During the last minute of cooking, add 2 tablespoons of the garlic butter to the skillet. Once the butter is melted, use a large spoon to baste the steaks in it.

● Remove the steaks to a cutting board and allow to rest for 10 minutes. Slice the steaks against the grain and top with another pat of garlic butter and flaky sea salt. Serve with the spiced roasted potatoes.

Garlic Butter Steak & Potatoes

This is a weeknight rotation meal for me. It's insanely addicting with each bite, so watch out. The thinly sliced flank steak is cooked until tender in a skillet and then tossed in a rich caramelized sauce that's both sweet and salty. A bed of soft rice cradles the saucy beef for a meal that just says comfort.

Sauce

3 tablespoons reduced-sodium soy sauce or tamari

3 tablespoons honey

2 tablespoons oyster sauce

2 tablespoons rice vinegar

¼ cup beef broth or water

1 teaspoon sriracha

½ teaspoon freshly ground black pepper

1 tablespoon cornstarch

Beef Stir-Fry

2 tablespoons avocado or canola oil

8 ounces broccoli florets, cut small (about 2½ cups)

Kosher salt

½ yellow onion, thinly sliced

4 garlic cloves, grated

1 pound flank steak, thinly sliced against the grain

½ cup canned sliced water chestnuts

Freshly ground black pepper

Juice of 1 lime

For Serving

Cooked long-grain white rice

3 scallions, thinly sliced, for garnish

Sesame seeds, for garnish

PREP
15 minutes

COOK
20 minutes

SERVES
4

● **Make the sauce:** In a small bowl, whisk together the soy sauce, honey, oyster sauce, vinegar, beef broth, sriracha, pepper, and cornstarch. Set aside.

● **Make the beef stir-fry:** In a large skillet, heat 1 tablespoon of the avocado oil over medium-high heat. Add the broccoli and cook until lightly browned, 2 to 3 minutes. Add ¼ cup water and cover the pan. Let the broccoli steam until just tender, another 3 to 4 minutes. Season with salt and remove to a plate.

● Return the pan to medium-high heat and add the remaining 1 tablespoon oil. Add the onion and garlic and cook until softened, 3 to 4 minutes.

● Meanwhile, pat the beef dry with paper towels and season with salt. Add the beef in one layer, being sure not to crowd the pan (you may need to do this in batches). Allow the beef to brown nicely, 2 to 3 minutes per side.

● Add the sauce to the pan and stir to coat the beef. Bring to a simmer over medium-high heat and allow the sauce to thicken slightly.

● Add the water chestnuts, return the broccoli to the pan, and toss everything to combine. Season to taste with black pepper and drizzle with the lime juice.

● **To serve:** Serve over white rice and garnish with the scallions and a sprinkling of sesame seeds.

Better-Than-Takeout Beef & Broccoli

These are a main course kind of wing, if you know what I mean. I love making these on game day, when they're always part of the spread. Make them in advance or serve them up during the party—let's be real, I'm usually cooking rather than paying attention to whatever team is playing. The food is always the real competition of a game day party, and I'm here to win.

Chile Sauce

1 tablespoon avocado oil

2 garlic cloves, grated

1 (1-inch) piece fresh ginger, peeled and grated

3 Thai red chiles, minced

3 tablespoons tamarind paste

2 tablespoons reduced-sodium soy sauce or tamari

¼ cup (packed) light brown sugar

2 tablespoons rice vinegar

Juice of 1 lime

1 tablespoon cornstarch

Kosher salt

Wings

Canola oil, for frying

½ cup all-purpose flour

¼ cup cornstarch

1 teaspoon baking powder

1 teaspoon paprika

Kosher salt and freshly ground black pepper

2 pounds chicken wings, tips removed, drumettes and flats separated

Thinly sliced scallions, for garnish

Sesame seeds, for garnish

PREP
15 minutes

COOK
40 minutes

SERVES
4 to 6

● **Make the chile sauce:** In a medium saucepan, heat the oil over medium heat. Add the garlic, ginger, and Thai red chiles and cook until softened, about 2 minutes.

● Add the tamarind paste, soy sauce, brown sugar, vinegar, and lime juice. Bring to a simmer over medium heat.

● In a small bowl, mix the cornstarch and 2 tablespoons water until smooth. Add to the saucepan and whisk together. Allow to simmer until thickened to the right consistency, another minute or two. Season with salt to taste.

● **Cook the wings:** Set a wire rack in a sheet pan and have near the stove. Pour 2 inches of canola oil into a large Dutch oven or heavy-bottomed pot and heat over medium-high heat to 350°F on a deep-fry thermometer.

● In a large bowl, whisk together the flour, cornstarch, baking powder, paprika, and salt and pepper to taste.

● Working in batches, dredge half of the wings in the flour mixture. Place in the hot oil and fry until lightly golden, 5 to 7 minutes—they won't be cooked all the way through. Using tongs or a fry spider, remove them to the wire rack and repeat with the remaining wings.

● Increase the oil temperature to 375°F on the deep-fry thermometer—depending on your current heat setting on the stove, you may need to increase the heat to medium-high or high.

● Again working in batches, add half of the wings to the oil and fry until deep golden brown and crispy, 4 to 5 minutes. Remove to a large bowl and fry the remaining wings until crispy. Add the sauce to the bowl and toss until evenly coated.

● Garnish the wings with thinly sliced scallions and sesame seeds.

Crispy Thai Chile Chicken Wings

SIDE PIECES

Say hello to Frisky Fries. I oven-bake the potatoes and load everything up on a sheet pan for easy, grazing-style sharing. If you're short on time, use frozen fries (it can be our little secret). With layers of gooey blue cheese fondue, Buffalo chicken, and spicy homemade ranch, they'll have you licking your fingers—they're so damn good.

Fries

3 medium russet potatoes (about 2 pounds), cut into a little less than ½-inch-thick matchsticks

3 tablespoons avocado oil

1 tablespoon cornstarch

1 teaspoon kosher salt

Cooking spray, for the pan

Buffalo Chicken

¼ cup hot sauce

2 tablespoons unsalted butter

1½ cups shredded rotisserie chicken

Blue Cheese Fondue

2 tablespoons unsalted butter

2 tablespoons all-purpose flour

1½ cups half-and-half

1 teaspoon kosher salt, plus more to taste

2 ounces cream cheese, at room temperature

¼ cup crumbled blue cheese (1 ounce)

Freshly ground black pepper

Assembly

2 celery stalks, diced

2 scallions, thinly sliced

¼ cup crumbled blue cheese (1 ounce)

1 tablespoon chopped fresh parsley leaves

Spicy Homemade Ranch (page 263), for dipping

PREP
15 minutes

COOK
15 minutes

SERVES
6

● **Make the fries:** Preheat the oven to 425°F. Place a baking sheet in the oven to preheat.

● In a large bowl, toss the potatoes, with the avocado oil, cornstarch, and salt to evenly coat.

● Carefully remove the hot baking sheet from the oven and lightly grease with cooking spray. Evenly spread the potatoes—you should hear them sizzle. Roast until golden brown and crispy, 35 to 40 minutes, flipping the potatoes halfway through.

● **Meanwhile, make the Buffalo chicken:** In a medium saucepan, combine the hot sauce and butter and whisk over medium heat until heated through and smooth. Add the shredded chicken and toss in the sauce. Allow the chicken to heat in the pot until warmed through, 3 to 4 minutes. Set aside and keep warm.

● **Make the blue cheese fondue:** In a medium saucepan, melt the butter over medium heat. Sprinkle in the flour and whisk until a paste forms. Slowly stream in the half-and-half and bring to a simmer. Simmer until the sauce has thickened and coats the back of a spoon nicely, 3 to 5 minutes.

● Remove from the heat and stir in the salt, cream cheese, and blue cheese. Whisk until the cheeses have melted and the sauce is smooth. Season with more salt and pepper to taste.

● **To assemble:** Remove the fries from the oven and toss one more time to loosen on the baking sheet. Top with the Buffalo chicken, blue cheese fondue, celery, scallions, blue cheese crumbles, and parsley. Serve with spicy homemade ranch on the side for dipping.

Frisky Buff-Chick Fries

These are for the olive-loving girlies. Now, those who think they don't like olives, beware, these will surely bring you over to the dark side. Pair them with a martini and they might just be the perfect definition of naughty.

4 ounces bacon (about 5 slices)

1 cup freshly crumbled Gorgonzola or blue cheese (4 ounces), warmed

1 teaspoon hot honey, plus more for serving

40 pitted Spanish green olives, patted dry

Canola oil or vegetable oil, for frying

½ cup all-purpose flour

2 large eggs, beaten

1 cup panko bread crumbs

¼ cup freshly grated Parmesan cheese

Kosher salt and freshly ground black pepper

Naughty Sauce (page 259), for serving

PREP
15 minutes

COOK
15 minutes

SERVES
4 to 6

● Line a plate with paper towels and have near the stove. In a large heavy-bottomed skillet, cook the bacon over medium heat until browned and crispy, 10 to 12 minutes, flipping halfway through. Drain on the paper towels and let cool to room temperature.

● In a small food processor, pulse the cooled bacon until very finely chopped. Add the Gorgonzola and hot honey and pulse again to a paste-like consistency. Place the mixture in a zip-top bag and cut a small hole in the corner of the bag.

● Line a baking sheet with paper towels. Pipe the cheese mixture into the olives and place on the prepared baking sheet. Be sure not to pat the olives totally dry, because the flour needs some moisture to be able to adhere well. Set aside until ready to fry.

● Line a second baking sheet with paper towels and have near the stove. Pour 2 inches of canola oil into a large Dutch oven and heat over medium-high heat to 350°F on a deep-fry thermometer.

● **Set up a dredging station with three shallow bowls:** Add the flour to the first and eggs to the second. In the third, stir together the panko and Parmesan. Season each bowl well with salt and pepper.

● Working in batches, dredge 5 to 8 olives in the flour, shaking off any excess, dip into the egg mixture, and lastly roll in the panko. Add the olives to the hot oil and fry until golden brown, 1 to 2 minutes. Remove with a fry spider or slotted spoon to the paper towels to drain.

● Drizzle with hot honey and serve with Naughty Sauce.

Fried Blue Cheese & Bacon-Stuffed Olives

This salad truly has my whole heart. It has a kiss of Asian flavors that has me saying "holy sh*t" with every single bite. I like to make a big batch and eat it out of the container right on the couch. Before I know it, the whole thing is gone.

1 English cucumber, cut into ½-inch-thick rounds

1½ teaspoons kosher salt, plus more to taste

2 tablespoons reduced-sodium soy sauce or tamari

2 tablespoons rice vinegar

2 tablespoons mirin

1½ teaspoons agave

1½ teaspoons Sweet & Spicy Chili Crunch (page 257)

1½ teaspoons toasted sesame oil

1 small Vidalia onion, thinly sliced

½ avocado, diced

1 teaspoon sesame seeds

PREP
15 minutes, plus marinating time

SERVES
4

• In a medium bowl, toss together the cucumber and salt and let sit for 30 minutes to tenderize the cucumber.

• Meanwhile, in a large bowl, whisk together the soy sauce, vinegar, mirin, agave, chili crunch, and sesame oil.

• After 30 minutes, rinse the cucumber and place it into the dressing with the onion. Toss to evenly coat and season with salt to taste. Marinate for at least 30 minutes and up to 3 hours in the fridge.

• Right before serving, add the avocado and sprinkle with sesame seeds. Serve at room temperature.

Marinated Cucumber & Sweet Onion Salad

Calling all my truffle lovers out there, you know who you are. Now, this recipe is perfect in the summer when fresh corn is at peak season. The natural sweetness of the corn with the distinct earthy flavor of the truffles is a flavor bomb of richness. There may be quite a bit of heavy cream added to round everything out. I'm so here for it.

2 tablespoons unsalted butter

1 large yellow onion, minced

3 shallots, minced

4 garlic cloves, minced

4 cups fresh corn kernels (from about 6 ears)

¼ cup dry white wine

2 cups heavy cream

3 tablespoons white truffle oil

1 tablespoon sugar

1 tablespoon kosher salt, plus more to taste

2 teaspoons freshly ground black pepper, plus more to taste

1 teaspoon fresh thyme

1 cup grated white cheddar cheese

2 ounces cream cheese, at room temperature

1 tablespoon minced fresh chives, for garnish

PREP
15 minutes

COOK
40 minutes

SERVES
4 to 6

● In a large pot, heat the butter over medium heat. Add the onion and shallots and cook until translucent, 5 to 6 minutes. Add the garlic and cook until aromatic, another 2 minutes.

● Add the corn and cook until the corn has softened slightly but is almost al dente in texture, 3 minutes or so. Deglaze the pot with the white wine and allow to reduce slightly, about 2 minutes.

● Stir in the heavy cream, truffle oil, sugar, salt, and pepper and bring to a simmer over medium-low heat. Add the thyme, cheddar, and cream cheese and stir frequently until melted. Reduce the heat to low and simmer until the creamed corn has further thickened and the flavors have melded, about 20 minutes.

● Transfer to a serving bowl, season with more salt and pepper to taste, and garnish with chives.

Truffled Cream Corn

These are truly the most addictive veggies you'll want to make any time of the year. They're definitely a requirement on the table during the holidays. I call this honey glaze my liquid gold—it's great on any root vegetable or squash in the colder months and makes them truly divine.

2 tablespoons unsalted butter, melted

1 tablespoon extra-virgin olive oil

2 tablespoons dark brown sugar

1 tablespoon honey

½ teaspoon fresh thyme

2 garlic cloves, grated

½ teaspoon kosher salt, plus more to taste

1 pound carrots, peeled and cut into 1-inch pieces

Freshly ground black pepper

2 tablespoons chopped fresh parsley, for garnish

Grated zest of ½ lemon, for garnish

Flaky sea salt, for serving

PREP
15 minutes

COOK
35 minutes

SERVES
6

- Preheat the oven to 425°F. Line a baking sheet with parchment paper.

- In a large bowl, whisk together the melted butter, olive oil, brown sugar, honey, thyme, garlic, and kosher salt until smooth and combined. It will be paste-like.

- Add the carrots and toss to coat. Spread the carrots evenly on the prepared baking sheet. Season with salt and pepper to taste.

- Roast until the carrots are almost tender and coated nicely in the glaze, 18 to 25 minutes, tossing halfway through.

- Serve garnished with parsley and lemon zest and sprinkled with flaky sea salt.

Candied Carrots

These potatoes are a jalapeño popper's easy best friend. They're too adorable and always ready to hang out. These baby potatoes are smashed and roasted to crispy perfection, then topped like a loaded twice-baked potato with chopped bacon and melted yellow cheddar, and studded with jalapeños.

1½ pounds baby Yukon Gold potatoes

4 tablespoons (2 ounces) unsalted butter

½ teaspoon garlic powder

½ teaspoon onion powder

½ teaspoon dried dill

½ teaspoon kosher salt, plus more to taste

Cooking spray, for the baking sheet

Freshly ground black pepper

2 medium jalapeño peppers, seeded and minced

6 slices bacon, cooked and chopped

1 cup grated yellow cheddar cheese

2 scallions, minced, for garnish

2 tablespoons chopped fresh cilantro leaves, for garnish

Naughty Sauce (page 259), for serving

PREP
20 minutes

COOK
1 hour

SERVES
4 to 6

- In a pot, combine the potatoes with water to cover. Bring to a boil over high heat and cook until fork-tender, 16 to 20 minutes. Drain and let cool until warm.

- Meanwhile, in a small saucepan, combine the butter, garlic powder, onion powder, dried dill, and salt. Let melt over low heat and stir to combine. Set aside.

- Preheat the oven to 425°F. Grease a baking sheet with cooking spray.

- Add the potatoes to the baking sheet, and using the bottom of a drinking glass, gently smash the potatoes until ¼ to ½ inch thick, making sure they are still able to hold their shape. Brush each potato with the melted butter mixture and season with pepper.

- Bake until very lightly golden brown on the edges, about 20 minutes, then flip the potatoes and brush again with spiced melted butter. Roast until deep golden brown with crispy edges, another 15 to 20 minutes.

- Top the potatoes with the jalapeño, bacon, and cheddar. Return to the oven and allow the cheese to melt, 4 to 5 minutes.

- Garnish with scallions and cilantro, and serve with Naughty Sauce.

Jalapeño Popper Potatoes

These taste just downright fancy; they give you that pinkies-up feeling any day of the week. If Blair Waldorf had an appetizer, it was these—truly a recipe any Upper East Sider would approve of. But let me tell you a secret: They're ridiculously simple to make. I use pancetta, aka fancy bacon, to add the sexy flair that pairs so nicely with the gooey Gruyère.

1 (4-ounce) package cubed pancetta

1 shallot, minced

1 garlic clove, grated

½ cup panko bread crumbs

1 teaspoon fresh thyme

Kosher salt and freshly ground black pepper

2 tablespoons chopped fresh parsley leaves, plus more for garnish

Grated zest of 1 lemon

Juice of ½ lemon

3 tablespoons extra-virgin olive oil

15 medium Baby Bella mushrooms, stemmed

½ cup grated Gruyère cheese

PREP
20 minutes

COOK
28 minutes

SERVES
8

● Preheat the oven to 400°F. Line a baking sheet with parchment paper.

● Line a plate with paper towels and have near the stove. In a large skillet, heat the pancetta over medium-low heat to render the fat slowly until the pancetta is browned and crisp, about 7 minutes. Using a slotted spoon, remove to the paper towels, leaving the drippings in the pan.

● Add the shallot and garlic to the pan and cook until softened, 3 to 4 minutes. Add the panko and thyme and cook, stirring frequently, until the bread crumbs are lightly golden, 2 to 3 minutes. Season with salt and pepper to taste and place in a medium bowl to cool slightly.

● To the bowl of panko, add the parsley, lemon zest, lemon juice, 1 tablespoon of the olive oil, and the cooled pancetta. Season with salt and pepper and mix to combine.

● Place each mushroom cap onto the prepared baking sheet and drizzle with the remaining 2 tablespoons olive oil. Season with salt and pepper. Stuff each mushroom cap with the panko mixture. Bake until the mushrooms just begin to turn golden brown, about 12 minutes.

● Remove from the oven and sprinkle with the Gruyère. Return to the oven and bake until the mushrooms are fork-tender and the cheese is melted, another 6 to 8 minutes.

● Garnish with additional parsley and serve.

Gruyère & Pancetta Stuffed Mushrooms

Let's get downright dirty. This cheesy bread is, dare I say this, tastier than the original from the famous pizza establishment? Yes. It. Is. This is one for the friends to end the night harmoniously in naughty fashion. Be sure to drizzle with hot honey or truffle hot sauce for extra decadence.

2 tablespoons yellow cornmeal

1 (13.8-ounce) tube refrigerated pizza dough (I like Pillsbury)

4 tablespoons (2 ounces) unsalted butter

2 garlic cloves, grated

1½ teaspoons garlic salt

½ teaspoon onion powder

1 cup grated yellow cheddar cheese

1 cup grated mozzarella cheese

For Serving

3 tablespoons finely grated Parmesan cheese

1 tablespoon chopped fresh parsley, for garnish

Marinara sauce, warmed

Truffle hot sauce (optional)

Hot honey (optional)

PREP
10 minutes

COOK
15 minutes

SERVES
6

● Preheat the oven to 400°F. Line a baking sheet with parchment paper.

● Dust the baking sheet with cornmeal and spread the pizza dough out evenly on top.

● In a small saucepan, combine the butter, garlic, garlic salt, and onion powder and melt over low heat, whisking to combine.

● Brush some of the butter mixture over the dough. Top the dough with the cheddar and mozzarella and drizzle with the remaining butter mixture.

● Bake until the cheese is melted and the crust is golden and cooked through, 10 to 13 minutes. Turn the broiler to high and broil until golden brown on top, 2 to 4 minutes.

● **To serve:** Sprinkle with the Parmesan and parsley. Cut the whole pizza in half. Then cut each half into 1-inch-thick sticks for dipping. Serve with warm marinara sauce, as well as truffle hot sauce or hot honey if desired.

The 4 a.m. Cheesy Bread

Let me introduce you to these mouthwatering potatoes: They're truly the love child of potatoes and cheese! Thinly sliced, creamy Yukon Golds are smothered in a blanket of three cheeses and a luscious sauce that will just melt in your mouth.

Softened butter, for the
baking pan

3 tablespoons unsalted butter

½ medium yellow onion,
thinly sliced

3 garlic cloves, grated

3 tablespoons all-purpose flour

1½ cups whole milk

1 cup chicken stock

1 tablespoon fresh thyme

1 teaspoon kosher salt

Freshly ground black pepper

1½ cups grated yellow cheddar
cheese

1½ cups grated Gruyère cheese

3 pounds Yukon Gold potatoes,
sliced ⅛ inch thick

½ cup freshly grated Parmesan
cheese

2 tablespoons chopped fresh
chives, for garnish

PREP
20 minutes

COOK
40 minutes

SERVES
8

● Preheat the oven to 400°F. Grease a 9 × 13-inch baking dish with butter.

● In a medium saucepan, melt the 3 tablespoons butter over medium heat. Add the onion and garlic and cook until softened, about 3 minutes. Sprinkle on the flour and stir to coat. Slowly stream in the milk and stock. Bring to a simmer over medium heat while whisking frequently, until the sauce has thickened and coats the back of a spoon nicely. Stir in the thyme, salt, and pepper to taste. Set aside.

● In a large bowl, combine the cheddar and Gruyère. Lay half of the potatoes down in the bottom of the prepared baking dish, top with half of the cream sauce and 1 cup of the mixed cheeses. Add the remaining potatoes, cream sauce, and cheese again to fill the baking dish. Sprinkle the top with the Parmesan.

● Cover with foil and bake until the potatoes are tender and the cheese is melted, 35 to 40 minutes. Remove the foil and preheat the broiler. Broil until golden brown and bubbling on top, another 2 to 3 minutes (watch carefully as all broilers vary).

● Allow to rest for 10 minutes before serving. Garnish with chives and serve.

Three-Cheese
Scalloped Potatoes

These sweet potato fries show up to party. This oven-fried method is truly incredibly life-changing, plus so easy to serve to a group at mealtime. It's a healthier way to make your favorite sweet and crunchy fries at home. Plus, the combo of sweet potatoes and Naughty Sauce is a match made in heaven for your mouth.

1¾ pounds sweet potatoes (about 4 medium), peeled and cut into matchsticks that are a little less than ½ inch thick

1½ tablespoons cornstarch

¼ teaspoon chipotle chile powder

½ teaspoon garlic powder

2 tablespoons avocado or canola oil

½ teaspoon kosher salt

Freshly ground black pepper

Cooking spray, for the pan

2 scallions, sliced, for garnish (optional)

Naughty Sauce (page 259), for serving

PREP
15 minutes

COOK
40 minutes

SERVES
8

● Preheat the oven to 425°F. Place a sheet pan in the oven to preheat.

● In a large bowl, toss the sweet potatoes with the cornstarch, chipotle powder, garlic powder, avocado oil, salt, and pepper to taste.

● Remove the baking sheet and carefully grease with cooking spray. Spread the fries in an even layer—you should hear them sizzle. Bake until golden brown, crispy, and tender on the inside, 35 to 40 minutes, flipping halfway through.

● Garnish with scallions and serve with lots of Naughty Sauce.

Chipotle Sweet Potato Fries

THE
CHERRY
ON
TOP

These are *those* cookies. Like middle-of-the-night, sneak-into-the-kitchen kind of cookies. You want to have one, but you'll end up eating half the jar. Crunchy on the outside and gooey on the inside, these brown butter chocolate chip cookies make the perfect bite that will melt your heart pieces.

16 tablespoons (8 ounces) unsalted butter

1¼ cups all-purpose flour

1¼ cups bread flour

1 teaspoon baking soda

½ teaspoon baking powder

½ teaspoon kosher salt

½ cup granulated sugar

1¼ cups packed light brown sugar

2 large eggs, at room temperature

1 large egg yolk, at room temperature

1 tablespoon pure vanilla extract

1½ cups bittersweet chocolate chips

PREP
25 minutes, plus chilling time

COOK
38 minutes

MAKES
16 cookies

● In a small saucepan, melt the butter over medium-low heat. Continue to cook while swirling frequently until the butter foams, is nutty in aroma, and golden brown in color, 7 to 8 minutes.

● Remove the browned butter to a heatproof bowl immediately to prevent it from burning and let it cool for 10 minutes. Place in the fridge to firm up until it's in a "softened" butter state while you prepare the rest of the ingredients.

● In a medium bowl, whisk together the all-purpose flour, bread flour, baking soda, baking powder, and salt. Set aside.

● In a stand mixer fitted with the paddle (or in a large bowl using a hand mixer), combine the "softened" butter, granulated sugar, and brown sugar and beat on medium speed until light and fluffy, 3 to 4 minutes. Add the whole eggs and egg yolk, one at a time, beating until incorporated after each addition. Add the vanilla and beat again until just combined.

● Gradually add the flour mixture, mixing until a dough forms. Remove the bowl from the stand mixer and fold in the chocolate chips using a rubber spatula.

● Refrigerate the dough covered or wrapped in plastic wrap preferably overnight, but for at least 2 hours, before baking.

● When ready to bake, preheat the oven to 350°F. Line two baking sheets with parchment paper.

● Scoop the dough into 3-tablespoon balls (1½-ounce cookie scoop) and place on the baking sheets about 2 inches away from each other.

● Bake one pan at a time on the center rack of the oven, until the edges are lightly golden brown but the center is still a little gooey, 12 to 14 minutes.

● Let cool on the baking sheet for 10 minutes, then serve warm or cool completely. Repeat with the remaining dough.

The Naughty Cookie

What happens when peanut butter and dates meet at a bar? These Snickers-inspired date treats, of course. They're the perfect little sweet treat to grab any time of the day. Dipped in sultry caramel and then decadent chocolate, they're layered with emotion all in one bite.

12 Medjool dates, pitted

¼ cup plus 1 tablespoon crunchy peanut butter

½ cup store-bought caramel sauce

6 ounces bittersweet chocolate, chopped

1½ teaspoons coconut oil

⅓ cup salted roasted peanuts, chopped

PREP
15 minutes, plus 20 minutes chilling time

MAKES
12 dates

● Line a small baking sheet or plate with parchment paper and set aside.

● Make a slit in the center of each date. Spoon about 1 teaspoon peanut butter inside. Dip each date into caramel sauce, letting any excess drip off. Place on the lined baking sheet and freeze for 10 minutes.

● Meanwhile, prepare a double boiler. Add 1 inch of water to a medium saucepan and place over low heat. Place a heatproof bowl on top and add the chocolate and coconut oil. Stir frequently until the chocolate and coconut oil melt and are smooth and combined.

● Remove the dates from the freezer and place a new sheet of parchment paper on the baking sheet. Dip the dates one at a time into the chocolate mixture, set on the new parchment, and immediately sprinkle with the chopped peanuts. You will want to move quickly here as the frozen dates make the chocolate set quickly.

● Freeze the dates again for 10 minutes to set, then serve.

● Store the dates in an airtight container in the fridge for a week or the freezer for up to 2 months. When storing in the freezer, be sure to thaw the dates for a few minutes until they are easy to bite.

Cocoa Caramel Crunch Dates

I think we're all looking for a relationship as beautiful as the one between peanut butter and jelly. I'm not sure one exists, but at least we have these cookies in the meantime. A buttery soft dough is studded with crunchy peanuts for allll the texture. That dough caresses the strawberry jam for a bite that brings back the nostalgic vibes.

Peanut Butter Cookies

1½ cups all-purpose flour

½ teaspoon baking soda

¼ teaspoon ground cinnamon

½ teaspoon kosher salt

8 tablespoons (4 ounces) unsalted butter, at room temperature

½ cup packed light brown sugar

¼ cup granulated sugar

1 large egg, at room temperature

1 teaspoon pure vanilla extract

1 cup creamy peanut butter

¾ cup finely chopped salted roasted peanuts

½ cup strawberry jam

Peanut Topping

⅓ cup creamy peanut butter, warmed

⅓ cup powdered sugar, sifted

6 tablespoons whole milk

2 tablespoons finely chopped salted roasted peanuts, for garnish

PREP
20 minutes

COOK
12 minutes

MAKES
24 cookies

- **Make the peanut butter cookies:** Preheat the oven to 350°F. Line two baking sheets with parchment paper.

- In a medium bowl, whisk together the all-purpose flour, baking soda, cinnamon, and salt. Set aside.

- In a stand mixer fitted with the paddle (or in a large bowl using a hand mixer), combine the butter, brown sugar, and granulated sugar and beat on medium-high speed until light and fluffy, about 3 minutes.

- Add the egg and vanilla and beat until just combined. Add the peanut butter and beat until just incorporated.

- Slowly add the flour mixture and beat again until just combined, being careful not to overmix. Remove the bowl from the mixer and fold in the peanuts with a rubber spatula.

- Scoop the cookie dough by the heaping tablespoon onto the prepared baking sheet and roll into a ball. Press into the dough with your thumb to make an indent. Spoon ½ teaspoon of strawberry jam into the center.

- Bake until lightly golden brown and set in the center, 10 to 14 minutes, switching the pans between oven racks halfway through.

- Let cool on the baking sheet for 10 minutes, then move to a wire rack to cool completely.

- **Make the peanut topping:** In a small bowl, whisk together the warmed peanut butter, powdered sugar, and milk to combine. Drizzle over the cookies, sprinkle with finely chopped peanuts, and allow to set. Serve.

Peanut Butter & Jelly Lava Cookies

This cobbler has a special place in my heart. It's my grandmother's recipe, and it's truly the showstopper of any party. Simple to make with the jammiest of blueberry bases and a custardy cake-like topping, it provides so much to love in each bite. Top with some vanilla ice cream for a moment of childhood nostalgia.

Softened butter, for the baking dish

Blueberry Base

2½ cups blueberries, fresh or thawed frozen

Juice of ½ lemon

1 teaspoon vanilla extract

1 cup sugar

½ teaspoon all-purpose flour

1 tablespoon unsalted butter, melted

Batter

1¾ cups all-purpose flour

4 teaspoons baking powder

6 tablespoons sugar

5 tablespoons cold unsalted butter

1 cup whole milk

Crumble

1 (13.25-ounce) box vanilla cake mix

8 tablespoons (4 ounces) unsalted butter, melted

PREP
15 minutes

COOK
30 minutes

SERVES
8

● Preheat the oven to 375°F. Lightly grease an 8 × 8-inch baking dish with butter.

● **Make the blueberry base:** Add the blueberries, lemon juice, and vanilla to the baking dish. Sprinkle with the sugar and flour. Drizzle the melted butter over the top and stir everything to combine.

● **Make the batter:** In a medium bowl, stir together the flour, baking powder, and sugar. Using a pastry blender or two forks, cut in the butter until the mixture resembles coarse crumbs. Gradually add the milk and gently stir to form a batter. Set aside.

● **Make the crumble:** In a large bowl, mix together the vanilla cake mix and the melted butter until crumbles form.

● Spoon the batter over the blueberry mixture, spreading it out to cover most of the fruit. Leave a few small holes for the berries to peek through. Sprinkle the top with crumble.

● Bake until the topping is golden brown and a knife inserted into the center comes out with moist crumbs, 25 to 30 minutes.

● Allow the cobbler to cool slightly before serving warm.

Grandma's Blueberry Cobbler

This is for all of those bougie coffee shop lovers out there. I wanted to create a dense yet moist snack cake that's rich in banana flavor with pops of fresh blueberries in each bite. Dressed in a crunchy vanilla glaze, it's one of those snackable cakes that you'll be thinking about until you make it again.

Banana Bread

Softened butter, for the loaf pan

2 cups plus 2 tablespoons all-purpose flour

1 teaspoon baking soda

¼ teaspoon kosher salt

1 teaspoon ground cinnamon

8 tablespoons (4 ounces) unsalted butter, at room temperature

¾ cup packed light brown sugar

2 large eggs

2 cups mashed overripe bananas (about 5 bananas)

1½ cups blueberries

Blueberry Icing

1 cup blueberries

1 to 2 tablespoons granulated sugar

1 cup powdered sugar, sifted

1 to 2 tablespoons fresh lemon juice

PREP
25 minutes

COOK
1 hour
15 minutes

MAKES
1 loaf

- **Make the banana bread:** Preheat the oven to 350°F. Grease a 9 × 5-inch loaf pan with butter and line with parchment paper. Set aside.

- In a medium bowl, combine 2 cups of the flour, the baking soda, salt, and cinnamon. Set aside.

- In a stand mixer fitted with the paddle (or in a large bowl using a hand mixer), beat the butter and brown sugar on medium-high speed until light and fluffy, 3 to 4 minutes. Add the eggs, one at a time, beating well after each addition. Add the banana and mix until just incorporated.

- Add the flour mixture and beat again on medium-low speed until everything is combined.

- In a small bowl, toss the blueberries with the remaining 2 tablespoons flour. Gently fold into the banana bread batter (this prevents the blueberries from sinking). Pour the batter into the loaf pan and smooth the top.

- Bake until golden brown and a toothpick inserted in the center comes out with a few moist crumbs, 1 hour to 1 hour 10 minutes.

- Let the loaf cool in the pan for 10 minutes, then remove to a wire rack to cool completely.

- **Make the blueberry icing:** In a small saucepan, combine the blueberries and 1 tablespoon of the sugar and cook over medium-low heat until the berries break down and the juices slightly thicken, 3 to 4 minutes. Taste and adjust the sweetness of the blueberry mixture by adding another tablespoon of sugar. Simmer another minute to allow it to fully dissolve.

- Remove the saucepan from the heat and strain the mixture through a fine-mesh sieve into a bowl. Set aside to let the blueberry compote cool completely.

Iced Blueberry Muffin Banana Bread

● Once cooled, add 2 teaspoons of the blueberry compote to a medium bowl with the powdered sugar and 1 tablespoon of the lemon juice and whisk to combine. The icing should be easy to drizzle. Add another tablespoon of lemon juice as needed. Store the remaining compote in an airtight container in the fridge for up to 4 days. I like to spoon it onto yogurt or toast.

● Spoon over the cooled loaf and allow the icing to set. Slice and serve.

Iced Blueberry
Muffin Banana
Bread, page 238

Matilda's
Chocolate Cake,
page 242

This chocolate cake is just sinful. It's the most delightful punishment of cocoa flavor inspired by the one and only Bruce from *Matilda*. No force-feeding of this cake here. Rather, this chocolate ganache buttercream is so decadent that you'll actually want to get it all over your face.

Chocolate Cake

Cooking spray for the pan

¾ cup unsweetened cocoa powder, plus more for the pan

2 cups all-purpose flour

1⅔ cups granulated sugar

2 teaspoons baking soda

1 teaspoon baking powder

1 teaspoon kosher salt

2 teaspoons espresso powder

½ cup vegetable oil

2 large eggs, at room temperature

1 egg yolk, at room temperature

2 teaspoons pure vanilla extract

1 cup low-fat buttermilk, at room temperature

¾ cup hot coffee

Chocolate Ganache Buttercream

3 ounces semisweet chocolate, finely chopped

⅓ cup heavy cream

4 sticks (1 pound) unsalted butter, at room temperature

3 cups powdered sugar, sifted

¾ cup unsweetened cocoa powder

1½ teaspoons pure vanilla extract

Pinch of kosher salt

PREP
35 minutes

COOK
28 minutes

SERVES
8

● **Make the chocolate cake:** Preheat the oven to 350°F. Grease two 9-inch round cake pans with cooking spray and lightly dust with cocoa powder. Line the pans with parchment paper rounds and lightly grease the paper as well.

● In a large bowl, whisk together the flour, granulated sugar, cocoa powder, baking soda, baking powder, salt, and espresso powder. Set aside.

● In a medium bowl, whisk together the oil, whole eggs, egg yolk, and vanilla to combine. Make a well in the dry ingredients and add the wet ingredients into the center of the well along with the buttermilk. Whisk gently until a cake batter forms.

● Add the hot coffee and whisk one more time until incorporated. The batter will be on the thinner side. Evenly divide the batter between the two cake pans.

● Bake until a toothpick inserted into the center of the cake comes out clean, 23 to 26 minutes.

● Let the cakes cool in the pans for 10 minutes, then flip them out of the pan onto a wire rack to cool completely. Remove the parchment.

● **Make the chocolate ganache buttercream:** Place the semisweet chocolate in a large heatproof bowl. In a small saucepan, heat the cream over medium-low until steaming. Pour over the chocolate and let it stand for a couple of minutes. Stir everything to combine until the chocolate is smooth. Set aside to cool until warm.

● In a stand mixer fitted with the paddle, beat together the butter and powdered sugar until the sugar is incorporated. Add the cocoa powder, vanilla, and salt and beat on low until combined. Increase the speed to medium and beat until light and fluffy, 1 to 2 minutes, scraping down the sides of the bowl as needed.

Matilda's Chocolate Cake

• Reduce the speed again to low and add the warm chocolate ganache. Once added, increase the speed to medium and continue whipping until nicely incorporated and light in texture, another 1 to 2 minutes. Set aside.

• To assemble the cake, place the first layer of cake on a serving plate or cake stand. Trim the top of the cake if domed to be even. Spread a nice layer of frosting over the center. Trim the top of the second layer of cake if needed. Place upside down onto the first layer of cake. Frost the outside of the cake evenly. Slice and serve.

Oh, the dreamy espresso martini. Why ever choose between coffee, a cocktail, and dessert when you can have all three? This is the official triple threat of desserts, served in a coupe and best enjoyed after midnight.

4 large pasteurized eggs, separated

2 tablespoons cornstarch

1½ cups heavy whipping cream

⅓ cup sugar

2 tablespoons instant espresso powder, plus more for garnish

3 tablespoons vodka

1 teaspoon pure vanilla extract

6 ounces semisweet chocolate, chopped (about 1 cup)

Coffee beans, for garnish

PREP
15 minutes, plus chilling time

COOK
15 minutes

MAKES
about 3½ cups (Serves 4)

● Off the heat, in a medium saucepan, whisk together the egg yolks and cornstarch until a smooth paste forms. Add 1 cup of the heavy cream, the sugar, and instant espresso and mix well to combine.

● Place the saucepan over medium-low heat and bring to a simmer while constantly whisking, 2 to 3 minutes. Continue to cook until the mixture becomes thick like pudding, 3 to 5 minutes.

● Remove from the heat and gently stir in the vodka, vanilla, and chocolate until nicely combined and the chocolate has melted. Set aside to cool until warm.

● In a stand mixer fitted with the whisk (or in a large bowl using a hand mixer), beat the egg whites on medium-high speed until stiff peaks form, 2 to 4 minutes.

● Gently fold the egg whites into the slightly warm chocolate mixture. Divide the chocolate mixture among 4 coupe glasses. Cover with plastic wrap and refrigerate for 4 hours or up to overnight.

● When ready to serve, in a stand mixer fitted with the whisk (or in a medium bowl using a hand mixer), beat the remaining ½ cup heavy cream on medium-high speed until soft peaks form.

● Dollop the heavy cream on top of each coupe glass, dust with espresso powder, and garnish each with 3 coffee beans.

Espresso Martini Mousse

When I think of a cake with pure elegance, it's this caramel glazed pound cake. This is my grandmother's recipe, made with lots of love. It's dressed in the most over-the-top sweet and rich caramel icing that will make your taste buds smile.

Pound Cake

Softened butter, for the pan

16 tablespoons (8 ounces) unsalted butter, at room temperature

2 cups granulated sugar

6 large eggs

1 tablespoon pure vanilla extract

½ teaspoon kosher salt

2 cups all-purpose flour

Caramel Icing

1 (16-ounce) box light brown sugar

½ cup evaporated milk

3 tablespoons unsalted butter, at room temperature

1½ cups powdered sugar, sifted

PREP
20 minutes

COOK
1 hour
5 minutes

SERVES
8 to 10

● **Make the pound cake:** Preheat the oven to 325°F. Grease a 10-inch tube pan with softened butter.

● In a stand mixer fitted with the paddle, beat the butter and sugar and cream on medium speed until light and fluffy, about 3 minutes. Reduce the speed to low and add the eggs, one at a time, beating well after each addition. Add the vanilla and salt and beat again until just combined.

● Add the flour gradually and continue mixing on low speed until just incorporated. Evenly spread the batter in the prepared tube pan.

● Bake until golden brown and a toothpick inserted in the center comes out with moist crumbs, about 50 minutes.

● Let cool in the pan for 10 minutes, then remove to a wire rack to cool completely.

● **Make the caramel icing:** In a medium saucepan, combine the brown sugar, evaporated milk, and butter. Bring to a hard boil over medium heat and let the sugar dissolve, 4 to 5 minutes.

● Remove from the heat and slowly whisk in the powdered sugar until the icing is thickened but spreadable.

● Drizzle or spread over the pound cake and let set; this happens quickly. Slice and serve.

Caramel–Glazed Pound Cake

We love a little pecan pie action all year long. These pecan pie bars happen to have a kick—of bourbon. It's a little elevated twist that's sealed with a kiss of chocolate. Better yet, they're made into bars for a portable sweet treat to take on a walk or enjoy in the privacy of your car. We won't tell anyone.

Crust

Softened butter, for the pan

1½ cups all-purpose flour

⅓ cup packed light brown sugar

10 tablespoons unsalted butter, at room temperature

1 teaspoon kosher salt

Pecan Filling

2 large eggs

½ cup light corn syrup

1 teaspoon pure vanilla extract

3 tablespoons all-purpose flour

¼ cup packed light brown sugar

1 cup roughly chopped pecans

1 cup semisweet chocolate chips

3 tablespoons bourbon

PREP
15 minutes

COOK
37 minutes

MAKES
9 bars

● **Make the crust:** Preheat the oven to 350°F. Grease a 9 × 9-inch baking pan with butter, line with a piece of parchment paper that hangs over the sides.

● In a stand mixer fitted with the paddle (or in a large bowl with a hand mixer), beat together the flour, brown sugar, butter, and salt on medium speed until a crumbly dough forms. Evenly press into the prepared pan.

● Bake until lightly golden brown, 10 to 12 minutes.

● Let cool until warm. Leave the oven on.

● **Meanwhile, make the pecan filling:** In a large bowl, whisk together the eggs, corn syrup, vanilla, flour, and brown sugar. Add the pecans, chocolate chips, and bourbon and fold into the mixture with a rubber spatula.

● Pour evenly over the warm crust, return to the oven, and bake until the filling is set, 20 to 25 minutes.

● Let cool completely in the pan. Lift out using the parchment, cut into bars and serve.

Chocolate Bourbon Pecan Pie Bars

Who says a third in the relationship doesn't work? These brownies are a beautiful union of marshmallows, chocolate, and crunchy almonds—the perfect late-night treat that you may just eat the whole pan of. You can use your favorite nuts and even add caramel sauce or butterscotch chips for extra decadence.

Softened butter, for the baking dish

⅓ cup unsweetened cocoa powder, sifted

⅔ cup all-purpose flour

½ teaspoon kosher salt

¼ teaspoon baking powder

8 tablespoons (4 ounces) unsalted butter, melted and cooled

2 large eggs, at room temperature

1½ teaspoons pure vanilla extract

1 cup sugar

1½ cups semisweet chocolate chips

1 cup mini marshmallows

½ cup chopped salted roasted almonds

PREP
15 minutes

COOK
34 minutes

MAKES
9 brownies

● Preheat the oven to 350°F. Grease an 8 × 8-inch baking dish with butter and line with parchment paper.

● In a large bowl, whisk together the cocoa powder, flour, salt, and baking powder. Set aside.

● In a medium bowl, whisk together the cooled melted butter, eggs, vanilla, and sugar until combined and smooth.

● Make a well in the dry mixture and add the wet mixture to the center of the well. Gently fold until a batter forms. Add 1 cup of the chocolate chips and fold again to combine. Evenly spread the batter into the prepared pan.

● Bake until the edges have set and the top is crinkly, 22 to 24 minutes.

● Remove from the oven and evenly sprinkle with the remaining ½ cup chocolate chips, the mini marshmallows, and chopped almonds. Return to the oven to bake for another 7 to 10 minutes, until the chocolate has slightly melted and the marshmallows are lightly toasted.

● Allow to cool in the pan for 10 minutes, then slice and serve.

Rocky Road Fudge Brownies

Does anyone ever have leftover doughnuts? No. So when you want to make this recipe, just go buy them and a couple extra for snacking. This is the breakfast of champions, brunch of brunches, and even a great dessert. I love the blackberry jam and orange combo, but you can try pairing your favorite jam and citrus. Even Nutella would be delicious.

2 tablespoons unsalted butter, at room temperature, for the baking dish

12 stale glazed doughnuts (1 pound 14 ounces), cut into 2-inch pieces

5 large eggs

2 large egg yolks

2½ cups half-and-half

1 tablespoon pure vanilla extract

1 teaspoon ground cinnamon

½ teaspoon kosher salt

Grated zest of 1 orange

¼ cup blackberry preserves

Powdered sugar, for dusting

PREP
15 minutes, plus 1 hour chilling

COOK
45 minutes

SERVES
8

- Grease a 9 × 13-inch baking dish with the butter.

- If your doughnuts are fresh, toast them in a 300°F oven for 10 minutes until dried out.

- In a large bowl, whisk together the whole eggs, egg yolks, half-and-half, vanilla, cinnamon, salt, and orange zest.

- Add the doughnuts and stir to combine. Pour the doughnut mixture into the baking dish. Cover with foil and place in the fridge to soak for 1 hour.

- Preheat the oven to 350°F.

- Dollop the bread pudding with the blackberry preserves and transfer to the oven. Bake uncovered until the top is golden brown and the custard has set, 40 to 45 minutes.

- Let cool for 10 minutes before serving. Dust with powdered sugar.

Doughnut Bread Pudding

LET'S GET SAUCY

The condiment of condiments, if you're a spicy kind of person, is the complex marriage of spicy and sweet. It's always in my fridge, no questions asked. You can buy it from the store, but I must say making your own is too easy and also has more depth of flavor. Whatever the dish is, chili crunch can probably be paired with it. Each spoonful has garlic, red chile flakes, and shallot— total harmony.

1 cup vegetable or canola oil

10 garlic cloves, chopped

2 tablespoons red chile flakes

1 teaspoon smoked paprika

1 shallot, minced

1 teaspoon agave

2 teaspoons soy sauce

½ teaspoon kosher salt

PREP
10 minutes, plus cooling time

COOK
10 minutes

MAKES
about 1 cup

● In a medium saucepan, combine the oil, garlic, chile flakes, paprika, and shallot. Bring to a simmer over low heat until fragrant and deep red in color, 8 to 10 minutes.

● Strain the oil through a fine-mesh sieve set over a heatproof bowl. Transfer the strained chile flakes, shallot, and garlic to a smaller bowl to cool and crisp. To the hot oil, stir in the agave, soy sauce, and salt.

● Once the oil has cooled to room temperature, add the cooled garlic and red chile flake mixture and stir to combine. Store in an airtight container in the fridge for up to 2 weeks.

Sweet & Spicy Chili Crunch

This is the SAUCE I put on everything, no joke. It's like the relationship you've always dreamed of, hot and steamy but always with a hint of sweetness. Believe me when I say Naughty Sauce is the ideal match with anything.

1 cup mayonnaise

3 garlic cloves, minced

1½ tablespoon teaspoon honey

3 chipotle peppers in adobo sauce, plus 2 teaspoons adobo sauce (for a milder sauce, use just 1 to 2 chipotles)

Juice of 1 lemon

Kosher salt

PREP
5 minutes

MAKES
1 cup

● In a food processor or blender, combine the mayonnaise, garlic, honey, chipotle peppers, adobo sauce, and lemon juice. Blend until smooth and season with salt to taste. Store in an airtight container in the fridge for up to 1 week.

Naughty Sauce

If there's an MVP of sauces, this is it. Inspired by the famous golden arches condiment that's iconic in every way, it not only drips down a burger beautifully but is also delicious on sandwiches, salads, and even Mac Daddy Smash Tacos (page 129).

½ cup 2% Greek yogurt or mayonnaise

2 tablespoons ketchup

1 tablespoon dill pickle juice

2 tablespoons sweet relish

2 tablespoons yellow mustard

½ teaspoon onion powder

½ teaspoon garlic powder

1 to 2 tablespoons hot water

½ teaspoon kosher salt

Freshly ground black pepper

PREP
5 minutes

MAKES
about 1 cup

● In a small bowl, whisk together the yogurt, ketchup, pickle juice, relish, mustard, onion powder, and garlic powder. Add the water, a tablespoon at a time, and whisk to combine until the sauce is easy to drizzle. Season with salt and pepper to taste. Store in an airtight container in the fridge for up to 1 week.

Golden Arches Sauce

Yes, I took pesto to a new naughty level, apologies in advance. Take that incredible green nut, the pistachio, and throw it in. It adds a new level of richness you didn't know pesto could have. Use as you would any other pesto, just don't forget to lick the spoon.

⅓ cup pine nuts

⅓ cup salted roasted pistachios

1 garlic clove, peeled but whole

Juice of 1 lemon

2 cups packed fresh basil leaves

½ cup extra-virgin olive oil

1 jalapeño, seeded and minced, or a pinch of red chile flakes

½ cup freshly grated Parmesan cheese

Kosher salt and freshly ground black pepper

PREP
10 minutes

MAKES
1¼ cups

● In a small skillet, toast the pine nuts over medium-low heat until nutty in smell and golden brown, 3 to 4 minutes. Remove to a plate immediately to cool.

● In a food processor, combine the pine nuts, pistachios, garlic, and lemon juice. Pulse until everything is finely chopped. Add the basil leaves and pulse again until the leaves are chopped and everything is combined.

● With the machine running, slowly drizzle in the olive oil until the consistency is almost smooth with some texture.

● Add the jalapeño, Parmesan, and salt and pepper to taste and pulse one last time until well mixed.

● Transfer to a bowl and use immediately or store in an airtight container in the refrigerator for up to 1 week. When storing pesto, it's best to place a piece of plastic wrap touching the surface of the mixture to prevent the basil from oxidizing and turning brown.

Basil Pistachio Pesto

Meet my first true love, ranch dressing. I want to drizzle it on everything and maybe even bathe in it. This is my take on a homemade ranch dressing with a bit of spice. It's truly an addiction that you'll want to have in your fridge all the time.

● In a high-powered blender, combine the mayonnaise, sour cream, buttermilk, garlic powder, onion powder, hot paprika, chives, dill, jalapeños, and black pepper and blend until smooth. Season with salt. Store in an airtight container in the fridge for up to 1 week.

½ cup mayonnaise

½ cup sour cream

⅓ cup low-fat buttermilk, shaken

1 teaspoon garlic powder

1 teaspoon onion powder

¼ teaspoon hot paprika

2 tablespoons chopped fresh chives

2 tablespoons chopped fresh dill

¼ cup sliced pickled jalapeños, drained of excess liquid

¼ teaspoon freshly ground black pepper

Kosher salt

PREP
5 minutes

MAKES
1½ cups

Spicy Homemade Ranch

This sauce is inspired by one of my favorite Miami restaurants. Its doors are now closed, but its Sun Sauce was truly addicting. In its memory, I've made my liquid gold rendition and recommend it for dipping or drizzling on any protein with rice, swap it as the sauce on the Parmesan Herb–Crusted Salmon (page 197) or the Artichoke Dip–Stuffed Chicken (page 199), or eat it on pretty much anything—it's ridiculous.

● In a small bowl, whisk together, the mayonnaise, mustard, soy sauce, apple juice, cider vinegar, and lemon juice until smooth. Season with salt to taste. Store in an airtight container in the fridge for up to 1 week.

1 cup mayonnaise

1 teaspoon Dijon mustard

1 teaspoon reduced-sodium soy sauce or tamari

2 tablespoons apple juice

1 tablespoon apple cider vinegar

Juice of ½ lemon

Kosher salt

PREP
5 minutes

MAKES
1 cup

Liquid Gold Sauce

I'll let you in on a little secret, these pickled radishes or red onions are easyyyyy. A restaurant-worthy condiment I add to sandwiches, salads, tacos, pretty much everything. Choose either thinly sliced radishes or red onion to pickle here—I like giving you multiple options for your roster. Make a batch once a week to always have on hand. It's truly the best 10-minute condiment.

3 bunches radishes, thinly sliced on a mandoline (about 1½ cups), or 2 small red onions, thinly sliced

1 teaspoon mustard seeds

½ teaspoon lightly crushed black peppercorns

1 cup apple cider vinegar

1 tablespoon sugar

1 tablespoon kosher salt

PREP
5 minutes

COOK
5 minutes

MAKES
2½ cups

● In a large heatproof jar, preferably glass, place the radishes, mustard seeds, and peppercorns.

● In a medium saucepan, bring the vinegar and 1 cup water to a simmer over medium heat, about 3 minutes.

● Once simmering, add the sugar and salt and stir for 1 minute or until dissolved.

● Remove the saucepan from the heat and carefully pour into the jar, I like to use a funnel. Lightly cover the jar with the cap and allow the mixture to cool to room temperature.

● When room temperature is reached, the pickled radishes or onions can be served or refrigerated for up to 1 week.

Too Easy Pickled Radishes or Red Onions

If you love a creamy, peanutty, spicy, sweet, and salty sauce with an Asian flair that's divine with noodles, to toss in a salad, or as a dipping sauce for something crunchy, this one's for you. It's extremely addictive with each bite and packs a punch of unexpected flavors.

● In a large bowl, combine the ginger, garlic, peanut butter, lime juice, tamari, agave, and sriracha and whisk to combine. Add a tablespoon or so of water as needed to thin to the right consistency. Store in an airtight container in the fridge for up to 1 week.

1 (1-inch) piece ginger, peeled and grated

2 garlic cloves, grated

½ cup all-natural unsweetened peanut butter

Juice of 2 limes

3 tablespoons tamari

2 tablespoons agave

2 teaspoons sriracha

2 to 3 tablespoons hot water

PREP
10 minutes

MAKES
⅔ cup

Ginger Peanut Sauce

When it comes to any seafood, this is my prized sauce, the crème de la crème, if you will. It's silky smooth for dipping, schmearing, or spooning onto grilled, blackened, or fried seafood.

● In a medium bowl, stir together the mayonnaise, sour cream, dill, parsley, garlic, Old Bay, hot sauce, lemon juice, and agave. Season with salt and pepper to taste. Store in the fridge in an airtight container for up to 1 week.

½ cup mayonnaise

⅓ cup sour cream

2 tablespoons chopped fresh dill

2 tablespoons chopped fresh parsley

2 garlic cloves, grated

2 tablespoons Old Bay seasoning

1 tablespoon hot sauce

Juice of 1 lemon

1½ teaspoons agave

Kosher salt and freshly ground black pepper

PREP
10 minutes

MAKES
1 cup

Old Bay Cream Sauce

ACKNOWLEDGMENTS

This cookbook would not have been possible without the help and support of so many incredible people in my life!

First and foremost, I want to express my deepest gratitude to the Naughty Fork community. I can't thank you enough for being part of this journey. Whether you've tried my recipes, shared your thoughts, sent messages of encouragement, or simply followed along, you have played a huge role in shaping my path and inspiring me to keep creating.

This cookbook exists because of you—because you believed in my vision, encouraged my creativity, and joined me in celebrating the joy of cooking. Your excitement has pushed me to experiment, refine, and share my passion in ways I never imagined. I am endlessly grateful for this community, and I truly wouldn't be here without you. This book is for you as much as it is for me.

To my friends, thank you for being my willing taste-testers and for giving me honest, thoughtful feedback. Your encouragement (and patience through endless recipe variations) helped shape this book into something truly special. And a very special shout-out to my Edgy Girls who have been especially involved in the tasting process. Your honest feedback, willingness to drop everything and come over multiple times a week to taste-test, and creativity in brainstorming fun concepts and innuendos made this journey even more special. I couldn't have done it without you!

To my family, your support has meant everything to me. Thank you for trying my recipes, cheering me on, and always believing in my passion for food. Your love and encouragement have fueled my creativity in the kitchen and have gotten The Naughty Fork to where it is today. I would not have been given the opportunity to write a cookbook without you.

A very special thank you to Laura Arnold for her invaluable contribution in co-writing this book and tirelessly testing the recipes with me. Your creativity in the kitchen, dedication to each recipe, and passion for good food made this book possible. I am incredibly grateful for all the time, energy, and love you poured into this book!

A huge thank you as well to Layla Schlack for her expert editing. Your ability to see my vision, give thoughtful feedback, and work together to ensure the book was something I was overjoyed to share with the world means everything to me. I am beyond grateful for the care you took in shaping this work into something truly special.

Thank you to my agent, Molly Pitzele, and manager, Mack Davey, who believed in me from the very start. Thank you for dedicating your time, creative ideas, and expertise to this project. Your guidance and support were pivotal in bringing this book to life. I'm so lucky to have you both by my side.

A big thank you to my book agent, David Doerrer, for your invaluable role in making this dream a reality. Your industry expertise, guidance, and commitment were key in bringing this project to fruition, and I couldn't have done it without you.

And lastly, a special shout-out to my dog, Kingston, for always being by my side—offering kisses and cuddles when things in the kitchen get frustrating. From your impeccable timing when cheese miraculously falls to the ground to your cameos on camera, this community and I love you. Thank you for being the best little sous chef a cook could ask for!

INDEX